FINANCIAL
101
FREEDOM

HOW TO GET OUT OF DEBT, STAY OUT OF DEBT, AND INCREASE YOUR NET WORTH

FINANCIAL
101
FREEDOM

MITCH MELAN

Printed in the United States of America.
Library of Congress Control Number: 2019938531
ISBN: 978-1-94963-977-3

Book Design: Jamie Wise

To the financial services mentors I've had throughout the years, the clients that have put their faith and trust in me to get to their financial goals, and the people who will benefit from this book.

And to my parents, who taught me common sense when it comes to money management and gave me the tools to live a good, strong financial life.

TABLE OF CONTENTS

INTRODUCTION

Annual income twenty pounds, annual expenditure
nineteen, nineteen and six, result happiness.
Annual income twenty pounds, annual expenditure
twenty pounds ought and six, result misery.
—*Charles Dickens, 1849*

W hen you think of a financial advisor, what do you picture? Maybe you imagine some guy in an expensive suit and a big corner office working to make rich people richer while paying little to no mind to regular people—hard-working Americans just trying to get ahead financially.

You may think financial advising doesn't apply to you, either; you're too busy just trying to stay afloat to worry about the world of investments and everything that comes with it, made even more complicated by jargon that can sound like a foreign language. It's hard enough to pay your bills, take care of your kids, and put gas in your car.

I know what that's like. My parents, both educators, gave me a small-town, middle-class Midwestern life. They were prudent about their money—always saving for a rainy day. When they couldn't afford something they wanted, they put it on layaway, making small installments until they could finally bring the item home. It was as simple as that. But in this day and age, it's not nearly as easy to live so simply.

THE CHALLENGES OF GETTING AHEAD IN TODAY'S WORLD

Every day, we're bombarded by messaging about what we need to buy to "keep up with the Joneses"—in real life and on social media—and purchase our way to a better life: Upgrade our wardrobes, get that new car, invest in shiny appliances that can do it all. The world we live in today makes it almost too easy to make poor financial choices. Things that would have been completely out of reach for most of us are now more accessible than ever—but often at a price many of us can't afford to pay. You can head into the mobile electronics store and walk out with any phone you want, regardless of your income or savings. The catch? They'll saddle you with a monthly payment that will feel like it goes on forever.

Car dealerships advertise that for just $399, you can drive off the lot in a brand-new Lexus. If you have the cash—or a credit card you can put it on—you might think, *Why not?* But the payments you'll make, how long they'll last, and the interest you'll accrue in the meantime are all hidden in the fine print.

We live in a world of *now, now, now,* and get-rich-quick schemes seem to come at us from every angle. Everyone's heard some story about his or her friend's uncle's sister-in-law who doubled her money in six months through one investment vehicle or another. But I've never heard Warren Buffett or any of the world's wealthiest people say, "I got rich quick, and here's how I did it." If that ever happens, please let me know.

It's easy to fall prey to this and so many other financial pitfalls, especially without guidance. When you cave to instant gratification—especially when you don't have the cash in your account—you're going to pay significantly more. Putting the newest iPhone on a credit card, leasing that luxury vehicle with money you don't have, or entering into a deal that promises to make you tons of green in "no time flat" is almost always a recipe for trouble. That's not to say that all debt is bad, but it's all about making sure that if you do take on some debt, it's the right kind and it's for the right reasons.

Retirement also poses a big challenge. People are living longer than ever before, and that means their retirement savings have to somehow hold out, as well. They spend as much—or more—in retirement than they did working. There are two problems that come along with that reality: 1) As we

FOR MOST FINANCIAL PROBLEMS, THERE'S A WAY OUT.

age, we typically develop health problems that stop us from working like we used to; and 2) Inflation is always increasing—things cost significantly more every ten to fifteen years. When you're in retirement with a fixed income, it can be extremely difficult to keep up.

But there's good news, too: For most financial problems, there's a way out. There are tools to help you fix almost any challenge you might find yourself in. There are opportunities to consolidate credit card debt, instruments that can outpace inflation and reduce taxes, and even cars that last a lot longer than they used to—meaning you can pay them off and keep driving them for years down the road.[1]

---

1   Inflation is the rise in the prices of goods and services, as happens when spending increases relative to the supply of goods on the market. The information in this book should not be considered as tax advice. You should consult your tax advisor for information concerning your individual situation.

Employers also offer plans and tools to help you save—*that's all kinds of good news.* Ninety percent of the battle is knowing what resources are available to you to make sure you're using every weapon in your arsenal. And as businessman and philanthropist W. Clement Stone has been widely quoted as saying, "Little hinges swing big doors." Saving a few dollars here and there can have a massive impact on your financial future.

MY PATH TO FINANCIAL ADVISING

Nobody's born knowing this stuff. That's exactly why I got into financial advising. I was in my twenties, just starting my career as a gym teacher, and I knew I needed to save money. I was young and single, but I had goals for the future. I wanted to buy a house one day. I wanted to start a family. But I wasn't sure how to make it all happen.

Luckily, I met a friend who was a financial advisor, and he began giving me advice. I started saving and realized I had a passion for it. I began to understand that if I made smart choices today, I could be set for tomorrow, and I could achieve everything I wanted in life. I also recognized that many of my coworkers—other educators who had been in the profession for years—could use similar help and advice. They had worked their whole lives, but a lot of them just hadn't saved enough to retire. They weren't where they wanted or needed to be. I didn't want to be in that situation, and I wanted to help others escape it, as well. Most people make changes out of inspiration or desperation, and I was inspired not to be old and broke. And with the help of my friend, I knew I didn't have to be. I learned my colleagues didn't need to be, either. With a little work and foresight, they could retire and be comfortable for the rest of their lives.

I've been a financial advisor for almost three decades now. Eight out of ten of my clients are just regular folks—middle-class Americans just trying to pay their bills, put their kids through school, save for retirement, and keep up with inflation. They're people we would rub elbows with in a teachers' lounge, an office building, or at the local supermarket.

WE CAN ALL USE A LITTLE HELP NOW AND THEN

Many people don't think they need a financial advisor—they believe that the only people who need professionals have deep pockets. But we all can use a little help now and then. Think of it this way: Lots of financial bigwigs didn't always have a ton of cash saved. Many didn't wake up, get a good job, and suddenly end up with $500,000 in a retirement account. Along the way, they were advised, given a path. They met someone like me—a professional in the industry—or a friend, family member, or neighbor. Someone took them aside and said, "If you just make a couple of changes, the future could look a lot brighter." The talk and jargon in this industry, and the thousands of books out there on money, make it all seem pretty intimidating, and, frankly, that's the point. But most people don't need all of that; they need simple solutions to the questions and issues they're facing.

Those in Middle America don't have to be left in the cold. We all have the potential to make our money work for us, and it's not as hard as it seems. With a few choices about how you handle your finances, you can determine whether your later years are as golden as they should be. For example, whether you give in to instant gratification or choose to hold off in exchange for a better future is a huge indicator of how secure you'll feel when you're ready to stop working.

In these pages, we'll work on fixing any financial problems you might already have and put systems in place to help you achieve your financial goals, no matter what they are. You'll find real-life analogies, not nonsensical industry jargon. We'll keep it simple because that's what most of us really need. And with chapters organized by the typical phases we go through in life, you can head to the section that applies to you, whether you're looking to buy your first home, shore up your retirement fund, or make sure your family is taken care of after you're gone.

The benefits of working on your finances are big: Once your money is in order, you'll find that you'll have less stress in other areas of your life. There won't be nearly as many worries to keep you up at night, and any struggles stemming from money—in your career, your relationships, and with your family—may improve.

While there's no overnight fix, especially for problems that have grown over the years, if you're willing to be honest with yourself, do the work, and stay disciplined, there's a way out and up, and I'm here to help you get there.

Let's get started building you a better financial tomorrow, today.

CHAPTER 1

IT'S EASIER THAN YOU MIGHT THINK

There's no doubt about it, managing your finances can be intimidating. And facing any money issues that have cropped up—especially over a long period of time—can be overwhelming. New clients regularly walk into my office, nervous to share all that they're dealing with. They have a lot of bills and even more debt. Often, they haven't saved a lot of money, even over the course of a ten-, twenty-, or thirty-year career. Plus, since the average American changes jobs ten to fifteen times over the course of their working lives, there are often different employer-sponsored accounts to track down—a 401(k) here, an IRA there.[2] They're worried there's just no

---

2   Alison Doyle, "How Often Do People Change Jobs?" *The Balance Careers*, October 17, 2018. www.thebalancecareers.com/ how-often-do-people-change-jobs-2060467

solution, and on top of that, they're embarrassed about the situation they've gotten themselves into.

Don't be intimidated or embarrassed. None of us has lived a financially perfect life, myself included. When I was in college, I took out a credit card—mostly to get the free T-shirt—but I didn't really understand how credit cards worked. Along with the T-shirt, I thought I had basically been offered free money. Pretty soon, I had run up a big bill, just having fun. And I wasn't paying the whole balance off every month; I was just hitting the minimum. When I looked at my statements more closely a few months down the line, I saw that I owed a ton of money and that the balance was continuing to skyrocket. On top of my spending, the card had a high interest rate, and that interest was compounding each time I failed to pay down the balance. I hadn't realized what I'd done. It took work, a lot of effort, and a bunch of extra cash to get out of debt. But when I finally faced the music, I was able to get it done.

Here's the flip side: When I was twenty-three years old, I started saving $100 per month. Every time I got a raise or I paid something off, I added that extra income to the $100 I was socking away. Because I was saving the money slowly, and only adding to the pot when I had a little extra coming through, I didn't even notice it. A decade or so later, I took a look at my accounts and I was astounded at how much money I had. Even better, the whole process had been pretty painless.

We're trained not to talk about money in our culture. It makes us uncomfortable. It's considered impolite. Plus, people don't want to reveal the mistakes they've made. But disclosing the facts is the first step to finding your footing and getting to a better place.

One of my clients, Shelly,[3] is a perfect example. The first time

---

3   I will never use actual client names here.

she walked into my office, I could tell Shelly, a teacher in her late forties, was anxious. She sat in front of my desk, looking down at her hands. "How can I help you?" I asked.

Shelly said, "I've gotten myself into some debt. And I'm just not sure how to get out."

"What's the situation? How much debt do you have?" I asked. She was shy at first, reluctant to reveal just how bad the situation had become. "It's nothing to be ashamed of," I told her. "A lot of people get into all kinds of situations with debt. But we have to look at the problem if we're going to find a solution. It's really the only way to fix it."

Slowly, she opened her bag and pulled out a stack of credit card statements.

It had happened little by little over time—a few hundred dollars here and there—but it had added up. She had numerous different credit cards, each with a different interest rate, and most of those rates were pretty high. She hadn't realized when she opened a card at her local Macy's or Target to get 10 percent off purchases that the interest would be so high. And when her bank offered her a card with a 0 percent interest rate to start, she signed up right away and failed to notice that, after a year, that rate jumped to 24 percent. She was paying just a bit more than the minimum each month as she tried to stay ahead of her other bills: keeping the lights on, putting food on the table, and other basic necessities. But the $150 she was putting up each month—just $20 over the $130 minimum—was barely putting a dent in the interest.

Thanks to those high interest rates, and the fact that almost all of her income went toward her basic needs, each month the credit card bills shot up higher and higher. And because she had so many cards, she could barely keep track of everything she owed.

On top of that, Shelly's car had recently broken down, and she'd bought a new one with a high monthly payment—in part because her credit score was low. She was struggling to keep up with that, too.

"I just don't know what to do anymore." She said it so quietly that I almost couldn't hear her.

Until that moment, she had been trying to do it all herself. She was a single woman who had been through a divorce, and when she had been married, she never handled any of her family's financials—her husband took care of it all. Now, on her own, she felt completely lost.

"We can figure this out. And it will be easier than you think," I told her.

We started with the credit cards, transferring all of that debt onto a single card that had a 0 percent interest rate for eighteen months. That meant she could get to work on making those payments without more interest adding up as she was paying her debt off overall. With just one credit card payment to make each month, she wasn't overwhelmed by as many bills.

When the cards had been consolidated and she was actually paying less to knock out that debt, she could put more toward her vehicle payment, chipping away at it so that less interest would build up over time. All good news.

The better news? Shelly called me the other day to tell me that in just three years she will be totally debt free.

In the meantime, we've been working on her retirement. Much of her retirement savings were sitting in cash—thousands of dollars earning just half a percent of interest. So, we diversified her money, moving it around, so that she would get a greater return on the cash she already had. In addition, every time she gets a pay raise or pays off a credit card, we take that extra money and put it toward her retirement account, so she's saving for her future while paying off her bills.

Shelly didn't have to make any huge life changes to achieve these results. While we did determine that she had to pay a little more attention to her budget, spending less on unnecessary items, she didn't have to move out of her home, find a smaller place, or drastically change her life—she just had to think about what she wanted. She determined that getting out of debt and living comfortably after her career ended were most important to her, and with some simple changes, she will be able to achieve those goals. Remember, little hinges swing big doors. It's up to you: What kinds of doors do you want to open?

SIMPLE SOLUTIONS

There's no magic pill for any of this, but for the most part, the strategies are simple. To help build a healthy financial life, you need to spend less than you make and save as much as you can. You try to avoid getting into debt, and if you do, you seek out a solution as quickly as possible.

What's the easiest tweak there is when you're dealing with credit card debt? Head to the dollar store, get yourself a pair of scissors, and cut up every credit card you have but one—you don't need six. Once that's done, consider these five simple tips that make getting out of debt, and avoiding it in the first place, a real possibility.

1) LIVE OFF CASH, NOT CREDIT

One of the simplest ways to avoid debt is to use cash, not credit. Credit cards are, basically, just selling money—and often at a crazy premium. And it's much easier to spend on plastic; you don't feel it until you get the bill. Instead, buy things you can afford and pay for them on the spot. Otherwise, you end up paying for them many times over in the form of interest. If you do have to put something on a card, make sure you're aware of your interest rate and work to pay it off quickly.

2) TAKE DOWN CREDIT CARD DEBT

Shelly's case seemed completely overwhelming, but it was actually pretty simple. Many of the millions of Americans with multiple credit cards and lots of debt can start with an easy switch: transferring that debt to just one card with zero or low interest. The result is just one bill each month. And with zero percent interest, all the money you're paying toward the bill goes to the principal—or the original amount charged—rather than to interest rates that never decrease.

3) YOU DON'T NEED TO GO COLD TURKEY TO SPEND LESS

Sometimes, it's the little things in life that keep you going—a hot cup of coffee from the shop down the street or a meal at your favorite restaurant where they already know your order. You don't have to give up all the small pleasures, but cutting back a little, and putting the cash you save toward your debt or retirement, makes a big difference. Shelly chose to eat out fewer times per month and spend less money on clothing. She didn't cut out those things entirely, but by purchasing less, she was able to pay off her bills faster and save more toward retirement, ensuring she could keep up her quality of life once she was no longer working.

4) MAKE SURE YOUR RETIREMENT ACCOUNT IS WORKING FOR YOU

Shelly's retirement account wasn't working nearly as hard for her as it could have. But with a few small shifts, we diversified it so that she could earn more on the money she was already saving (more on that later in Chapter 4). A quick conversation with a financial advisor can help you make the switch, too, and it means you don't have to get deep in the weeds of the many options available to you to get the most benefit. You can leave that part to the professionals.

5) MAKE A DOLLAR, SAVE A DIME

Another simple switch that Shelly made—and that you can do, too—was to make sure her raises really paid off by using those increases toward credit card bills and saving for retirement. If you take half that raise and put it toward your bill, while investing the other half in a retirement account—boosting your contributions every month—you'll be in a better situation later on. A lot of people I work with pay 10 percent of their income to their church. If you made yourself a similar priority and allotted an additional 10 percent to yourself, you'd be setting yourself up for a very comfortable future.

This isn't rocket science, and I try to predicate my career on the "KISS Method": Keep It Simple, Stupid. You'll find the same logic throughout this book. If you go to the doctor for an earache, you just want something to eliminate the pain. You don't need to know the chemicals in the drops he or she prescribes, or to be familiar with the drug company that made it, or the lab where it was tested. Most of my clients are very busy nowadays and they're not interested in knowing all the details—and they don't have to. They come to advisors to get answers—to get where they want to go. That's what you'll get here. My philosophy is if you're driving your Toyota Camry at the speed limit in the center lane, then you're going to get wherever you're going just fine. We'll never take the more complicated route if we don't have to. And along the way, you'll discover that, for the most part, managing your money and building the life you want is easier than you may think.

Some situations, however, are a bit more complex. Without in-depth knowledge of how finances work, people can end up in some pretty tricky situations. While there's usually a light at the end of the tunnel, it might take longer—and a lot more work—to get there. In the next chapter, we'll look at some of the worst financial situations I've seen and talk about how the clients and I dealt with the issues at hand.

CHAPTER 2

IT'S HARDER THAN YOU MIGHT KNOW

While the principles necessary to build a healthy financial life are fairly simple, without the right knowledge or assistance, it's very possible to get into challenging situations that are hard—if not impossible—to resolve. Small mistakes add up over time, until they become insurmountable. And, frequently, people wait until it's too late to take action. It's as if their kitchens are flooding and they hold off on calling a plumber until the water reaches their chins.

NOT ALL FINANCIAL MISTAKES ARE FIXABLE

Unfortunately, not all financial mistakes are fixable, and even one poor choice can have a huge impact on the rest of your life. Take

Terry, for example. Terry had been a public-school math teacher for most of his career. He'd seen hundreds of students master the concepts he taught in his classes and go on to graduate and lead successful lives. Terry was also only a year away from receiving his full pension: 60 percent of his salary, which he would get every year for the rest of his life after he retired.

But that year, Terry decided he was ready for a change. He was lonely—his wife had passed away a few years earlier—and he wanted to be closer to his daughter and his grandchildren, who lived a few states away. On a whim, he applied for a new position at a school near his daughter's home that paid a little more money, and when he was offered the job, he took it.

Terry resigned from the school where he had spent almost all of his working years and withdrew all of the money in his pension to pay off some bills and fund his move. However, he didn't realize the full impact of his decision. Instead of sticking around for another year, and claiming a retirement check in excess of $35,000 annually for the rest of his life, Terry received a lump sum of $150,000, which, after taxes, amounted to about $110,000. If he had waited just one more year before making his move and lived for another thirty years, that $35,000 annually would have added up to $1,050,000. In the end, he gave up more than a million dollars for just $110,000. Doesn't seem like a fair trade, does it?

It was the equivalent of being at the one-yard line, and just kneeling down till the clock ran out. He was so close to the end zone, but he didn't bring the ball through. Why? He didn't understand the impact of his decision.

While the lump-sum payout had seemed large at the time—especially since his salary had topped out at around $60,000 per year—the money was going fast, and Terry came to my office for advice on how he could keep and save more. I had the unfortunate responsibility of telling him what he could have had if only he had held onto his previous position for another year, essentially reaching the end zone. Terry sat in my office, obviously in shock as I explained the situation. He was completely unaware of how catastrophic his decision had been. Most of his money—and the opportunity to make it last for life—was gone, period.

While there is often a way out when it comes to many of the financial challenges people grapple with, for this one, there was no real solution. Terry's only option was to work for as long as he could to get a pension equal to 20 percent of his salary. Terry's case illustrates just how much the money decisions we make matter, often more we think. Sometimes, it's just impossible to get toothpaste back in the tube. You can't always make up for time or money spent, and usually, by the time people realize the impact of their choices, it's just too late.

SOMETIMES, IT'S JUST IMPOSSIBLE TO GET TOOTHPASTE BACK IN THE TUBE. YOU CAN'T ALWAYS MAKE UP FOR TIME OR MONEY SPENT.

Take the case of another client of mine, Maria. Maria had come to me for years to get help managing her finances. Sadly, she passed away after a long illness. But Maria had been a careful planner throughout her life and had worked hard to leave money behind for her daughter, Amy. After Maria's passing, Amy received a substantial inheritance—about $200,000. But at nineteen years old and with no real financial experience, Amy didn't know how to properly save or spend. Within three years, she had burned through all of the money her mother had left her. It had seemed like an endless supply of cash when the check first came in, but after a few years of living above her means there was just nothing left.

When she came to me to develop a financial plan, she would be starting from scratch. Had she invested even a portion of her inheritance, she would have been able to build a comfortable life for herself for years to come. The charts that follow show how much Amy's money could have grown if she had invested just half of her inheritance.

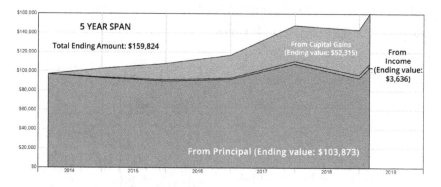

Actual investment earnings on $100,000 over 5 years. The Growth fund of America A (AGTHX) 3/1/2014 - 2/28/2019 (11.5% rate of return) Americanfunds.com

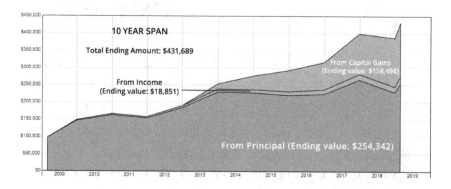

Actual investment earnings on $100,000 over 10 years. The Growth fund of America A (AGTHX) 3/1/2009 - 2/28/2019 (15.5% rate of return) Americanfunds.com

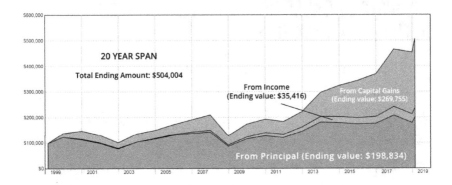

Actual investment earnings on $100,000 over 20 years. The Growth fund of America A (AGTHX) 3/1/1999 - 2/28/2019 (8.5% rate of return) Americanfunds.com

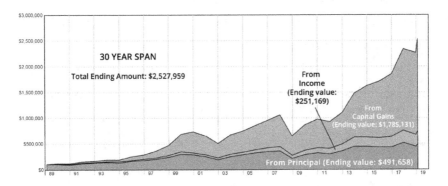

Actual investment earnings on $100,000 over 30 years. The Growth fund of America A (AGTHX) 3/1/1989 - 2/28/2019 (11.5% rate of return) Americanfunds.com

All investment entails inherent risk. Investment return and principal value will fluctuate so that an investor's shares, when redeemed, may be worth more or less than their original cost. Current performance may be higher or lower than the performance illustrated. Actual results do not reflect the deduction of advisory fees, brokerage or other commissions, or any other expenses that a client would have paid and also may not reflect the reinvestment of dividends and other earnings. While there is no assurance that a diversified portfolio will produce better returns than an undiversified portfolio, and it does not assure against market loss, a diversified portfolio may reduce a portfolio's volatility and potential loss.

THE BIGGEST CAUSE OF UNFIXABLE FINANCIAL MISTAKES? A LACK OF KNOWLEDGE

Terry and Amy's circumstances were different, but the financial issues that arose from them stemmed from a common place: a lack of knowledge. A lack of knowledge is almost always at the root of unfixable mistakes. I can't tell you the number of times people have sat in my office, lamenting that if only they had known the consequences, they never would have made the choices they did.

The financial crisis of 2008 provides numerous examples of how a lack of knowledge can be catastrophic. In an environment where buying property was easier than ever, millions of people purchased homes they couldn't afford with adjustable-rate mortgages that eventually took up a significant portion of their take-home pay. Limited financial literacy was at the root of many of those decisions: people didn't understand the terms of their loans, and that the seemingly low rate they received upon signing would fluctuate significantly. As the value of their homes went down, their mortgage rates went up, and they found themselves in a disastrous situation.

Pete was one of those individuals. In the early 2000s, Pete took out loans with what appeared to be great rates to flip houses and get into the rental property market. He bought a number of properties—some he flipped, others he used for rental income. Things were going fine until 2008 hit. Suddenly, the homes he was flipping were worth a lot less than he had paid for them. The $2 million in property he leveraged was worth about half that amount, and the interest rates on his mortgages kept climbing. To make matters worse, because of high rates of unemployment and the dismal job market, many of his tenants couldn't afford to pay their rent. Without that rental income, and with no real opportunity to get back the money he had invested, he had to go down the road of foreclosure and bankruptcy and find himself a regular job.

Crashes like that in 2008 can also be catastrophic for people handling their investments on their own, without much knowledge of how the market works. Tom Lewis, retired CEO of Realty Income Corporation, a successful real estate investment trust, once said, "The American stock market is similar to watching a person walk up the stairs with a yo-yo. People focus on the yo-yo going up and down, while the real story is the consistent movement of the person up the stairs."[4] Turning on the news during a bad year and hearing about all kinds of volatility without an awareness of the bigger picture—that the market trends upward overall—could make anyone go insane. But instead of consulting a professional during turbulent times, many people panic when their investments lose value. They move all of their money to conservative funds that seem safer, but earn significantly less. When the market recovers (and it's almost guaranteed to do so), their money is on the sidelines. So, not only do they miss out on growth from the rebound, but they can't ever make up what they lost.

SOME CATASTROPHES CAN BE TEMPORARY

Thankfully, not all financial mistakes are completely catastrophic. While finding the light at the end of the tunnel will most likely require a professional, there is usually an opportunity to build a better future. The Wilsons learned this lesson when they found themselves $45,000 deep in credit card debt. Enough paper cuts can bleed you to death, and that's how it had happened for this family.

---

4   "Tom Lewis Once Had a Great Quote about the American Stock Market," *The Conservative Income Investor*, July 11, 2014. https://theconservativeincomeinves-tor.com/tom-lewis-once-had-a-great-quote-about-the-american-stock-market/

Little charges here and there on multiple cards added up over time, and with high interest rates on most of them, the Wilsons were soon drowning in debt.

With so much to pay back, few assets, and relatively low incomes, they would never have been able to tackle it all on their own. Their only option was to bite the bullet and file for bankruptcy. With a debt-consolidation bankruptcy program, they were able to pay their debts back over time and work to repair their credit. They also had to do a 180-degree turn on their spending habits and their lifestyle. Through serious effort and discipline, they went from being major consumers, using credit cards to buy things they couldn't afford on a regular basis, to serious savers who only made purchases when they had cash on hand. If you're willing to learn from your mistakes and put in the work, there is likely a route to a better place.

My client Denise serves as a perfect example. She made some poor choices when it came to her pension, but because she sought help, she was able to get back on track. Denise was trying to do the right thing. She had a lot of credit cards, many with high balances and interest rates, and she thought that if she could just pay some of them down, she'd be in a better financial position. However, instead of attempting to roll the balances over to a low-interest or no-interest card and chip away at the debt, she took money out of her pension to pay those balances off—without really understanding the consequences. By withdrawing from her pension, she had taken a big bite out of her retirement savings.

But all wasn't lost. Denise was relatively young—in her early forties—and so she had the opportunity to replace the money she withdrew by saving more each month on a pre-tax basis and putting it back into her pension. We developed a plan for her to do this effectively, which included bumping up her contributions each time she got a raise. She had to be more diligent about her spending and work harder to save, but in the end, it was worth it. She was able to put back what she had taken out and retire right on time.

Sometimes it's not necessarily about changing your habits so much as it's about uncovering previously unknown tools and resources to get out of debt and manage other financial challenges. Tanya learned this when she and I began working together. When I met her, she had more than $70,000 in student loans. Completely overwhelmed by her five-figure debt, Tanya figured that she would just spend the rest of her life paying off her loans bit by bit—making the minimum payment each month as the interest continued to grow.

Little did she know, because of her government job, her middle-class income, and her role as head of her household, she could enroll in the Public Service Loan Forgiveness Program. Those working for government or nonprofit organizations have the opportunity to apply for this program, which eliminates the balance of their Direct Loans after they make one hundred and twenty qualifying payments—about ten years' worth.[5] As part of this program, she would pay as little as $200 per month for ten years, and afterward, her loans would be completely forgiven. She would end up paying about 25 percent of what she would have paid with interest over the life of her loans, and could take those savings and invest them in building a better life for her family.

---

5   "If you are employed by a government or not-for-profit organization, you may be able to receive loan forgiveness under the Public Service Loan Forgiveness Program," *Federal Student Aid*, https://studentaid.ed.gov/sa/repay-loans/forgiveness-cancellation/public-service.

FINDING A WAY OUT AND UP

In certain instances, with the proper knowledge and support, there's not only a way out, but also a way up. Tanya's situation is a perfect example, as things were about to get even better for her. After we resolved her student loan debt, we were able to address her other financial issues. Tanya had some credit card debt that she had been struggling to pay down. Since she was only in her thirties, she had plenty of time to bolster her retirement account. So, we borrowed on it to pay off her high-interest balances. That improved her credit score, which allowed her to refinance her home and receive a lower interest rate—meaning she'd pay less money for her home overall.

I also advised that she continue to drive her vehicle, which was nearly ten years old but in good working condition, since it had already been paid off. By maintaining her vehicle, she was able to take the money she'd be putting toward a new car payment and, instead, create an emergency fund. And with this cushion in place, she didn't have to depend on credit cards to cover big purchases.

IN CERTAIN INSTANCES, WITH THE PROPER KNOWLEDGE AND SUPPORT, THERE'S NOT ONLY A WAY OUT, BUT ALSO A WAY UP.

Tanya was able to fix four problems at once: solving her student loan issues by tapping into the benefits of the Public Service Loan Forgiveness Program; paying off credit cards that were racking up about 20 percent in interest; paying herself back and further bolstering her retirement plan, thanks to lower rates on her credit cards and home loan; and building up an emergency fund so that she didn't need to rely on credit cards in the first place.

Tanya had no idea that any of these options were available to her, and if she hadn't sought help, she probably wouldn't have been able to address the challenges she faced in such an effective way. In her situation, seeking support—and gaining knowledge in the process—made all the difference.

Sometimes making the choice to meet with a financial advisor to help improve financial health rather than to remedy a specific ailment can be *all* good news—news you might not have received otherwise. Occasionally, clients come in with the simple goal of better managing their financial lives, and I'm able to uncover funds they didn't even know existed. People have come into my office seeking a plan for retirement or looking for help saving for a vacation home, and I've found accounts from old employers with $250,000 or $300,000, or more in them due to generous matching programs that my clients were unaware of.

How does this happen? How do you lose track of hundreds of thousands of dollars? With the average person holding the same job for just about four years before switching roles, according to the Bureau of Labor Statistics, people often rack up multiple retirement accounts over the course of a lifetime.[6] They move on to a new opportunity without looking back, and imagine that their old account has been rolled into their new one, or occasionally forget about old funds entirely—especially if they relocate and those account statements continue to go to their previous address. When I can track down an account like that, people tend to look at me like I walk on water, but it's simply about knowing where to look.

---

6   "Employee Tenure Summary," *United States Department of Labor Bureau of Labor Statistics*, September 20, 2018, www.bls.gov/news.release/tenure.nr0.htm.

BREAKING DOWN BIG CHALLENGES

In all of these cases, my clients' troubles—and the occasional surprise windfall—didn't arise due to carelessness; they came from a lack of knowledge. Those surprised by the amount they had in lost accounts had been missing out on money that was rightfully theirs because they had no idea it was there. And for the most part, those who found themselves struggling under difficult financial circumstances were earnest, hardworking people who just didn't understand what they were getting themselves into with each financial choice they made.

While no one gets into financial struggles on purpose, there are steps you can take to avoid big problems in the first place and address money issues if they do come up. Here are two key points to keep in mind:

DON'T BE AFRAID TO SEEK HELP

When things start to get ugly, waiting to get help often makes a bad situation worse—even though waiting is all too common. People hesitate to act because they're too intimidated or embarrassed to seek assistance, though they're far from alone.

Financial systems can be challenging to understand, and they're further complicated with jargon meant to exclude regular people. When you don't have the tools to properly address a financial situation on your own, or you're just not sure of the next step to take, a financial advisor can be the answer. An advisor's goal—and role—is to help people fix the financial problems they're not capable of solving on their own. You'd visit a dentist for a root canal or a mechanic to fix your carburetor, and you can—and should—consider using a financial advisor in the same way. If you're up against something you can't handle yourself, don't be afraid to seek help.

A good advisor will help create a roadmap to success—or at least identify a path out of the woods. If you're facing circumstances that seem insurmountable, an advisor might be the way to go.

A LITTLE KNOWLEDGE GOES A LONG WAY

But often, a little knowledge goes a long way—especially if the situation isn't dire. The key to life is learning. If you can access the information to make decisions confidently, then you're guaranteed to be in a better spot than if you just charge forward blindly. If you're looking for strategies on how to manage your financial life in general, I'm here to help. Going forward, we'll dive into the challenges, opportunities, and solutions that arise at every stage of life—from financing an education and navigating that first job, to ensuring loved ones are covered long after your last breath. First, we'll address a big concern for most American families: financing an education.

CHAPTER 3

FINANCING AN EDUCATION

I f you're planning to pay for higher education for yourself, your spouse, or your children, you've probably done some thinking (or worrying) about how to manage what is likely to be an exorbitant price tag. For the 2018–19 school year, the average annual cost of tuition in America was $9,716 for public colleges and universities, and a whopping $35,676 for private institutions.[7] And worse, the cost continues to increase at a breakneck pace. Post-secondary education has one of the highest inflation rates of any product in the country, increasing about twice as fast as the general inflation rate.[8] And the expense has significantly outpaced wage growth—advancing

---

7   Farran Powell, "See the Average Costs of Attending College in 2018–2019," *US News and World Report*, September 10, 2018. www.usnews.com/education/best-colleges/paying-for-college/articles/paying-for-college-infographic

8   "Tuition Inflation," *FinAid.org*. www.finaid.org/savings/tuition-inflation.phtml

almost eight times faster than wages did between 1989 and 2016.[9] These factors make financing a degree one of the toughest challenges most families face today.

It's a lot to take in, but—as with most things in life—having a strong plan is the way to make it through. Fortunately, there are plenty of options available to help you save, as well as creative solutions that you may not have considered. In this chapter, we'll discuss some of the tools to make paying for school less painful. But first, it's crucial that you get your priorities straight.

THERE'S ONLY SO MUCH TO GO AROUND

Imagine embarking on a home-renovation project. You probably wouldn't demolish part of the kitchen, rip out the carpet and wallpaper in your bedrooms, and begin tiling the bathroom all at once, then leave everything half done when you run out of resources faster than you anticipated. Ideally, you'd save up for a particular project, complete it, cross it off your list, and then make sure you have the funds necessary to keep going before moving on to the next room. Why? Because for most of us, there are only so many assets to go around.

As such, whether you're renovating your home or addressing your financial needs, you have to hone in on what's most important to you, make *that* your focus, and take steps to get it done before you tackle the next thing on your list. Each family has its own circumstances and corresponding financial priorities—whether it's saving for retirement, ensuring there's a plan in place for long-term care,

---

9   Camilo Maldonado, "Price of College Increasing Almost
    Eight Times Faster Than Wages," *Forbes,* July 24, 2018.
    www.forbes.com/sites/camilomaldonado/2018/07/24/
    price-of-college-increasing-almost-8-times-faster-than-wages/#bcdb08966c1d

bolstering an emergency fund, or paying for an education. But it can be difficult to keep individual priorities in mind when emotions are involved.

Truthfully, it's a lot easier to sell a college plan than a retirement plan—even in cases when retirement should be the first priority. That's because guilt is a major player here. Most people put their kids' needs ahead of their own, and so they believe that if they have limited resources, it's best to put any available funds toward college. They worry that failing to save enough for their children's education makes them a bad parent, that it indicates that they don't love their kids enough.

In reality, the decision to fund college over retirement for the sake of the next generation is not so black and white. If you have a great pension and you know you're

THE DECISION TO FUND COLLEGE OVER RETIREMENT FOR THE SAKE OF THE NEXT GENERATION IS NOT SO BLACK AND WHITE.

going to be taken care of in retirement, perhaps helping your child pay for college is the right choice. But if putting up the cash to fund your son or daughter's education means you won't be able to support yourself as you age, you risk becoming a burden to them later on.

That's why—for most people looking to fund their children's education—determining how they'll pay for retirement should come first. You can always take out a loan to send your kids to college, buy a house, or purchase a car; you *can't* really take out a loan to retire. We've all heard about the perils of being "house poor"—owning a home and struggling to make ends meet due to the high cost of home ownership and everything else that comes with it. Well, it's possible to be "college-savings poor," too.

FIRST, CROSS RETIREMENT OFF YOUR LIST

If you're thinking about your children's future alongside your own, starting early can help you avoid this dilemma. If you can cross saving for retirement off your list before your first child is born, do it. While saving for retirement in such a short period of time may seem like a wild idea, it's often much easier than you think. Here's why: money set aside in a retirement fund continues to grow, whether you're adding to it or not. Once you've contributed a substantial amount of cash to that pot, you can then turn your attention—and the majority of your available assets—toward college savings.

Michelle was able to save for retirement as well as college, and achieve another aspiration she thought might be out of reach: staying home to raise her children when they were little. Michelle's parents were clients of mine, and they recommended that she come to see me shortly after she had gotten married. Michelle was only twenty-three, but she knew she wanted to be able to save for her own future and afford college tuition for her children—though she hadn't had them yet. She was passionate about these goals because of the example her parents had set.

Michelle had grown up with her mother at home, taking her to school each day and attending every dance recital and soccer practice, and it had meant a lot to her. She also didn't have to worry about student loan debt since her parents had worked hard to save for her education. They had also prioritized their own retirement and long-term care planning over the years and were living very comfortably on their own. As such, Michelle and her husband wouldn't have to spend a lot of time and money caring for her aging parents a few years down the line. Now that she was an adult and thinking about building a family of her own, Michelle wanted to do her best to provide her family with the kind of life and opportunities her parents had given her.

As a bookkeeper with a moderate income, Michelle feared that accomplishing these goals would be impossible, but she wanted to see what her options were. I thought she might be surprised by all that she could achieve with just a little planning. We ran the numbers and found that if she put $5,000 per year (or about $416 per month) into a Roth IRA for ten years—until she was thirty-five—she'd have about $1 million saved at age sixty, based on the average rate of return. If she had her first child when she was thirty-three, she could even stay home with him or her for the first few years, and *then* put all of her extra income toward college when she reentered the workforce, since her retirement would be covered.

If Michelle had waited to begin saving for retirement until she made more money or until her first child was born, setting aside funds for college while working to build up her savings would have been far more challenging. But by starting early with a clear goal in mind, she'll be able to have her cake and eat it, too.

If you do find yourself working toward both goals simultaneously, something most Americans grapple with, you can still make progress. But rather than splitting any extra funds equally between your priorities, I'd keep an 80/20 rule: contributing 80 percent toward retirement and 20 percent toward college. That way, you're making strides toward both goals without compromising your—or your children's—future.

PICK A PLAN THAT WORKS FOR YOU

Once you've determined your priorities and considered your retirement goals, the next thing to figure out is *how* you're going to pay for college. It's crucial to devise a plan that works best for you and your family. But not all plans are created equal.

I've seen parents put up tens of thousands of dollars for private school tuition, expecting that investing in their children's education up front would lead to a free ride to the elite college of their choice. While that plan might work out on occasion, I certainly wouldn't bank on it. That said, there are so many ways to save for college, and a less traditional option might be right for you.

A plan that's almost certainly not your best bet if you're planning to pay for your child's education? Taking out a loan on his or her behalf. For example, lots of families choose to take out a Parent PLUS loan, a federal loan available to parents of dependent undergraduate students. These loans have higher interest rates and fees than do Direct Loans, which are made directly to students.[10] When you take out a Parent PLUS Loan, you essentially co-sign for your child's education, and you're on the hook for that loan, no matter what. If it's for a significant amount, making those high monthly payments could prevent you from being able to retire. And if health issues crop up, you may end up inadvertently requiring your child to foot the bill for your expenses later on—which could far exceed what they'd pay if they were to take out their own loans.

Another potentially upsetting outcome with Parent PLUS Loans? If your child decides to drop out of school at any point, or take a job unrelated to their studies—in retail, for instance—you could be in a situation where, thanks to interest, you're paying twice what you borrowed without much to show for it. It would be like purchasing tickets for a seven-day vacation to Australia and ending up at your local theme park for the afternoon instead, with no way to

---

10 "Parent PLUS Loan Overview," *Edvisors*. www.edvisors.com/college-loans/federal/parent-plus/introduction-to-federal-parent-plus-loans/

recoup your expenses. Of course, there's no way to predict the future, but there are many other, more sustainable, routes to pay for school, and almost all of them come with less to regret if your child ends up choosing a different path than the one you imagined (or paid for). Below are a handful of options to make saving for an education easier to swallow.

529 PLANS

If you're saving for a child's education, a 529 plan—or "qualified tuition plan"—can be an excellent option. These are explicitly for education savings and come with a slew of benefits that can lift much of the burden from worried parents' shoulders. There are two types of 529 plans: prepaid tuition plans and education savings plans.

PREPAID TUITION PLANS

Most prepaid tuition plans are sponsored by individual states, and allow you to purchase credits toward future college tuition and fees, locking in current rates—a great benefit considering the ever-escalating price of higher education. These plans are exempt from federal taxes, and often from state and local taxes too, sweetening the deal a little more.

However, there are some limits to prepaid tuition plans. Credits can only be purchased at participating schools, which are usually public and located in the state where the plan is purchased. In addition, these plans often require that the account holder and/or beneficiary live in that state when the account is opened. Plus, funds are usually restricted to tuition and mandatory fees; they can't be used for expenses such as room and board.[11] What happens if you or your child chooses a non-participating institution—like a private school or one located in another state? The plan typically pays the average cost of an in-state public school, while you're responsible for the rest.[12]

While there are certainly pros and cons to prepaid tuition plans, if you are planning to reside in your state for the long haul and send your child to a local college or university, this might be a good option for you.

EDUCATION SAVINGS PLANS

Also sponsored by states, education savings plans are investment accounts meant to be applied to education expenses, including tuition, fees, and room and board. They can be used at any higher-education institution, including schools outside of the country, and for up to $10,000 in tuition at primary and secondary schools as of 2018. Since education savings plans are investment accounts, you can choose between different types of portfolios, including ones that start out with an aggressive approach and become more conservative as the beneficiary reaches college age.[13]

The funds you contribute to education savings plans grow tax free, and as long as they are applied to qualified expenses, they are not subject to federal tax when you withdraw them. Many states also offer tax benefits for residents who have a state-sponsored plan. However, it's important to note that if funds are used for expenses that aren't considered "qualified," they are taxed at that federal and state level,

---

11 "An Introduction to 529 Plans," *U.S. Securities and Exchange Commission*, May 29, 2018. www.sec.gov/reportspubs/investor-publications/investorpubsintro529htm.html

12 "Section 529 Plans," *FinAid.org*. www.finaid.org/savings/529plans.phtml

13 Ibid.

and incur a 10 percent federal tax penalty.[14] With more flexibility than a prepaid tuition plan, tax advantages, and the potential for significant growth, education savings plans are almost always a good bet.

Note that there are fees associated with both prepaid tuition plans and education savings plans, including enrollment and administrative fees. For education savings plans, fees can be reduced or waived in certain cases, such as maintaining a large balance, making automatic contributions, or residing in the state offering the plan.

Another benefit? For both types of plans, account balances can be rolled over to another beneficiary. If you have two children, and one is not able to use any or all of the funds because he or she receives a scholarship or chooses not to go to school, then you can use the balance for another child. Elena and Mark experienced this firsthand. When they had their first child, they began saving for college, putting as much money as they could into an education savings plan each month. When their second child was born, they didn't have to worry about saving quite as much, since their first account was well funded and they knew they would be able to roll over any extra money into their younger child's account. Even better, their first child received a full ride to play soccer at his first-choice school, so they were able to transfer all of the funds into their second child's account and cover the entire cost of her education with funds from the plan.

Contributions to these accounts can also be made by anyone, so grandparents and other family members or friends can lend a hand and help boost the balance. Small contributions also add up over time; while a few hundred dollars for birthdays or the holidays might not seem like much, they can make a big difference down the line.

---

14   Ibid.

529 plans are especially beneficial if you start saving—you guessed it—early. Opening these accounts when a child is born or when just a few years old gives the money plenty of time to grow and weather any market shifts (remember Tom Lewis's analogy of the yo-yo headed up a set of stairs?) and allows you to capitalize on tax benefits, too.

Note that participation in a 529 College Savings Plan (529 Plan) does not guarantee that contributions and investment return on contributions, if any, will be adequate to cover future tuition and other education expenses or that a beneficiary will be admitted to or permitted to continue to attend an educational institution. Contributors to the program assume all investment risk, including potential loss of principal and liability for penalties such as those levied for non-educational withdrawals.

An investor should consider, before investing, whether the investor's or designated beneficiary's home state offers any favorable state tax treatment or other state benefits such as financial aid, scholarship funds, and protection from creditors that are only available for investments in such state's qualified tuition program. Consult with your financial, tax or other adviser to learn more about how state-based benefits (including any limitations) would apply to your specific circumstances. You may also wish to contact your home state or any other 529 college savings plan to learn more about the features, benefits and limitations of that state's 529 college savings plan. Furthermore, the Tax Cuts and Jobs Act that was signed into law on December 22, 2017 allows for up to $10,000 a year per beneficiary in tax free distributions from a 529 Plan if used for tuition incurred for enrollment or attendance at a public, private, or religious elementary or secondary school. Check with your state's guidelines prior to withdrawing the funds.

For more complete information, including a description of fees, expenses and risks, see the Plan's offering statement or program description.

MUTUAL FUNDS

A 529 plan is not your only option. If you're not sure what the future holds for your child and you want to avoid any penalties in case they receive a large scholarship or choose not to attend college at all, then you can invest in a mutual fund, which doesn't come with the same education-based restrictions that a 529 plan carries.

A mutual fund is simply a portfolio made up of different investment options, such as stocks and bonds, run by a money manager. People participate in a particular fund by buying shares of it, and any losses or gains are distributed among all participants. The structure of these types of funds makes them less risky than picking stocks and bonds as an individual—especially if you have limited knowledge of investing.[15] Mutual funds allow you to grow your money without much experience or work; the fund manager takes care of all that. Though, since it's an investment account, there is no guarantee that your money will grow.

There are also fees associated with mutual funds, as well as costs to buy and sell shares. There aren't any tax benefits with mutual funds, either, although avoiding that 10 percent penalty if your child doesn't need the money for school could be considered a benefit in and of itself.

---

15   Anne Sraders, "What Is a Mutual Fund? Pros, Cons, Types, and How to Invest," *The Street*, July 25, 2018. www.thestreet.com/personal-finance/what-is-a-mutual-fund-14658862.

TAPPING INTO AN IRA

While IRAs are meant for retirement savings, you can also use them to help finance an education, since there is no penalty on early withdrawals used to pay for qualified education expenses as long as they're for you, a spouse, child, or grandchild.[16] When it comes to taxation, there are some differences between traditional IRAs and Roth IRAs. With a traditional IRA, if you withdraw money before you reach age 59.5, contributions and earnings are taxed as ordinary income. For Roth IRAs, withdrawing your contributions won't incur any taxes, but taking out earnings will.[17] For example, if you contributed $30,000 toward a Roth IRA and it earned another $20,000 in interest, for a total value of $50,000, you could take out that original contribution of $30,000 tax free, but the $20,000 would be taxed. It's important to note that with either account, anything you withdraw might count toward your overall income, potentially affecting future financial-aid packages.[18]

DEPLOY YOUR RESOURCES STRATEGICALLY

No matter what savings plan you choose, you can increase its impact by deploying your resources strategically. When you pay off a bill or bring in more income, consider where those freed-up funds

---

16   Farran Powell, "5 Things to Know About Using an IRA to Pay for Tuition," U.S. News and World Report, March 30, 2016. www.usnews.com/education/best-colleges/paying-for-college/articles/2016-03-30/5-things-to-know-about-using-an-ira-to-pay-for-tuition.

17   Fidelity Learning Center, "Thinking About Using Your Retirement Savings to Pay for College?" *Fidelity*. www.fidelity.com/learning-center/personal-finance/college-planning/using-retirement-savings.

18   "Saving for College? Here Are Some Alternatives to the 529 Account," *The Wall Street Journal*, October 18, 2017, www.marketwatch.com/story/here-are-some-alternatives-to-the-529-college-savings-account-2017-10-17.

will make the biggest difference and distribute them accordingly. Say you recently paid off your car and suddenly you find yourself with an extra $400 every month. Dedicate that money toward your education savings account or mutual fund until it's time to purchase a new car. Similarly, if your child finishes a daycare program that came with a hefty monthly bill and enters a free public school, you can put the amount you were spending on tuition toward his or her college savings account. The same goes for work raises: allocate any income boosts toward your current financial priorities—whether you're working to pay off debts, add to your retirement account, and/ or contribute to a college fund (this may be the right time to employ the 80/20 rule we discussed earlier in the chapter).

GETTING A LATER START? ALL IS NOT LOST

Earlier is always better. But if you're getting a later start on saving, or you decide to go back to school yourself, there are still plenty of ways to finance an education. For example, families can take out a home equity line of credit, usually at a lower interest rate than other loans offer. We also discussed using IRA funds to cover tuition. Borrowing from a 401(k), or life insurance plan, to cover college or graduate school expenses or pay off loans may be a good choice, though every situation is different. If you're considering these options, weigh the pros and cons and proceed with caution to make sure you're not creating one financial burden in an attempt to address another.

DON'T HESITATE TO CONTACT AN EXPERT

When it comes to higher education, the rules and opportunities out there change frequently. If you're trying to determine the best option, sitting down with a school counselor or a professional specializing in this area—especially if you have a child nearing college age—is always a good idea. They can offer a unique insight into how a particular decision about saving, borrowing, or spending might affect your eligibility for financial aid, or introduce you to a new scholarship or grant program that you've never heard of before. An advisor can also help you uncover little-known benefits specific to your situation that can work to your advantage.

For example, one of my clients was going into a relatively obscure field, and there wasn't a relevant academic program in the state. Because her home state didn't offer a major in her area of interest, she was able to pursue the track she wanted elsewhere and still pay in-state tuition. The outcome for this particular client? Saving tens of thousands of dollars while going after her dream career.

SEE WHAT'S OUT THERE

While paying for tuition certainly comes with sticker shock, much like the situation above, there are numerous opportunities available in the education realm if you know where and how to look for them. Many high schools offer the option to take college courses, allowing students to rack up college credits and potentially graduate early, reducing tuition bills. You or your child may also determine that a traditional four-year college is not necessarily the right choice. Instead, a vocational or trade program might be a better fit for individual skills and interests and come at a much lower cost, while providing the skills to land a lucrative job as an electrician, mechanic, or cosmetologist. This is just another reason why it's worth looking at all of your options.

LOOK INTO LOAN FORGIVENESS OR REPAYMENT PROGRAMS

If loans are part of your payment strategy—a reality for many families, with Americans owing nearly $1.5 trillion in student loan debt—lots of graduates can take advantage of loan forgiveness or repayment programs.[19] The Public Service Student Loan Forgiveness Program, which we discussed in the previous chapter, helps those who qualify to essentially erase student loan debt by working full-time for a government or nonprofit organization for ten or more years. Parents who take out Parent PLUS loans and work for public–service organizations may qualify for loan forgiveness as well if they meet the same criteria.[20]

Some private-sector companies are also helping to pay off student loans as part of their benefits package, which can make a tremendous difference for graduates. For example, Aetna and Fidelity Investments match up to $10,000 in student loan payments for their employees.21 This is a hot trend in the realm of employer benefits, and it's likely that more companies will begin offering loan repayment as part of their packages to help attract new talent.

As you begin navigating higher-education costs, it's crucial to remember that every family's circumstances are different, and there is no perfect answer for how to afford what is bound to be one of the biggest expenses you'll face. However, many of the basic tenets of spending smart and saving well can also set you up to success-

19   Andy Talajkowski, "12 Companies Offering Student Loan Forgiveness Hiring Now," *Glassdoor.com*. August 10, 2018. www.glassdoor.com/blog/companies-student-loan-forgiveness/

20   "Public Service Loan Forgiveness Program," *Federal Student Aid*, December 2013. https://studentaid.ed.gov/sa/repay-loans/forgiveness-cancellation/public-service

21   Zack Friedman, "Student Loan Repayment Is the Hottest Employee Benefit of 2018," *Forbes*, October 18, 2018. www.forbes.com/sites/zackfriedman/2018/10/18/student-loan-repayment-employee-benefits/#2fca65dd566f

fully finance schooling. If you work to stay out of debt and build up emergency funds, then you'll have the flexibility to deploy your assets more effectively than if you're attempting to tackle high credit card bills and ever-mounting interest while putting money away for the future. Live below your means, pay yourself first, and save for retirement. Any extra funds you have can then go toward an education fund, in whatever form it takes. It's as simple—and challenging—as that.

Keep these concepts in mind as you begin strategizing and saving:

- No one has unlimited assets. You have to choose the priorities that matter most to you and go from there.

- In most cases, retirement should come first. While saving for college may seem most crucial—especially if you have children—you can't take out a loan for retirement. If you prioritize education savings and don't put enough away for your future, you could be creating a big burden for your family down the line.

- Don't be afraid to get creative. 529 plans are a great way to save for higher education, but you can also use other vehicles, such as mutual funds and IRAs. And don't overlook scholarships, grants, and loan forgiveness or repayment programs when developing a plan to finance schooling.

- Be strategic about spending and saving. Your income and expenses will probably shift over the course of your life. Think about how to best deploy your resources for the biggest impact, putting raises or extra money toward your savings—college or otherwise.

- Don't hesitate to contact an expert. School counselors and financial advisors with expertise in financing an education can be very helpful in identifying resources and opportunities you may not have thought of. If you have any questions, make sure to reach out.

With some tools to handle the cost of an education, it's time to move on to one of the next milestones in many adult lives: landing a job, and navigating the income, benefits, and challenges that come with it.

CHAPTER 4

"I GOT A JOB!"

Getting a job is an important milestone for those just gradu-
ating college or entering a new field. It's an opportunity to
demonstrate your skills and work ethic, and do your part to
contribute to a company's success. But whether you're starting your
first job or your twentieth, you can rely on the same set of concepts
to help ensure that your employer—and the benefits they offer—will
work as hard for you as you'll work for them. Here, we'll talk about
the benefits many companies offer, where to seek alternative or additional coverage if necessary, and how to ensure that you're using all
of the resources available to you to help build your financial security
as best you can.

UNDERSTANDING YOUR BENEFITS

Whenever you begin a new role, the first thing to do is develop a strong understanding of your benefits. Every company has a different set of offerings, and it's up to you to make sure you have a clear picture of what's available to you, how to enroll in your plans, and any coverage or services that you may need to secure on your own to supplement your company's offerings.

On day one of your new job, before you set up your desk or pick up a set of pens from the supply closet—or even when you first receive that offer letter—contact HR for the lowdown on all of benefits and programs available to you. It may seem like a chore that can wait a few days or weeks, especially if your organization doesn't have a formal orientation, but don't delay this important step. If you do, you may find that a benefit you were counting on isn't actually available, and end up scrambling to come up with another option. Here are some of the offerings large companies typically provide as part of their benefit packages, as well as information on alternatives if you find that your organization won't give you everything you need.

HEALTH INSURANCE

Health insurance is often one of the first benefits that comes to mind when starting a new job, and most companies offer it. The US Bureau of Labor Statistics reported that as of March 2018, 69 percent of private-sector employees and 89 percent of public-sector employers had access to health care benefits through their jobs.[22] While a few employers cover the full cost of health insurance, many pay a portion and require that employees handle the rest. They often offer multiple

---

22 "Employee Benefits in the United States – March 2018," *US Bureau of Labor Statistics*, July 20, 2018. www.bls.gov/news.release/pdf/ebs2.pdf.

plans as well, with different options for coverage, allowing you to determine what to buy based on what you think you'll need.

If this is the case, you want to make sure to choose a plan that fits your circumstances. Some plans offer lower premiums (the amount you pay for the plan—usually per month) with higher deductibles (the amount you pay up front before your insurance begins paying), while other plans offer higher premiums with low or even nonexistent deductibles. If you are in good health and rarely get sick or visit the doctor, a low premium, high-deductible plan may be for you, since you'll save money on the premium each month and avoid paying much of the deductible if all goes well.

But if you have multiple medical conditions, see a series of physicians, and/or take multiple prescriptions to keep your health issues under control, it's probably better to pay more each month, with the knowledge that the majority of your visits and procedures will be covered. Choosing the right health insurance is a personal decision, and it's important to weigh the pros and cons of each plan available, along with your individual needs, before making a decision.

SHORT-TERM DISABILITY INSURANCE

Short-term disability is private insurance that provides some or all of your income for a specified period of time if you're unable to work due to injury or illness.[23] It is an important benefit that many employees overlook, especially if they're young and healthy. But it can be invaluable to you if you do have it—and put you in an extremely difficult situation if you don't—as Shonda quickly learned. Shonda began her job as an administrative assistant at a well-known firm, and because

---

23 "Short-Term Disability (STD) Insurance: The Basics," *Disability Benefits 101*, October 15, 2018. https://ca.db101.org/ca/programs/income_support/std/program.htm.

of the company's size and reputation, she figured her employer would offer a full slate of benefits, including short-term disability.

She had held positions at a few other companies—all of them smaller than her current employer—and short-term disability was always part of her benefits package. Over the years, she had seen colleagues take weeks off of work for surgeries without sacrificing much pay. She'd been to countless baby showers, wishing her colleagues well as they left to take twelve or more weeks of paid leave—part of which was covered by their short-term disability packages.

When, six months later, Shonda got pregnant with her first child, she didn't give it a second thought. She just assumed she'd be offered leave thanks to a short-term disability policy, just like the ones she'd seen her former co-workers take advantage of. But a few months into her pregnancy, when she reached out to her HR department to share the good news and talk about her plans to take some time off after her baby was born, she learned that short-term disability was not part of her benefits package.

> **IT'S A GOOD IDEA TO KEEP ENOUGH MONEY IN YOUR EMERGENCY FUND TO COVER THREE TO SIX MONTHS OF EXPENSES SO THAT YOU'RE PREPARED FOR THE UNEXPECTED.**

While she was eligible for time off thanks to the Family and Medical Leave Act, a US law that allows employees at qualifying companies to take up to twelve weeks of leave for family and medical situations without jeopardizing their jobs or losing their health insurance coverage, her company wasn't required to pay her during that time.[24] Like many families in America, Shonda's couldn't afford to go twelve weeks without a paycheck. With six months to go before the birth of their child, Shonda and her husband found themselves struggling to come up with ways to make up for Shonda's lost wages during the time she'd spend at home with her baby.

If you find out that short-term disability is not part of your benefits package, it is possible to purchase your own plan, which will provide you with coverage and peace of mind—especially if you end up having any health issues that keep you out of work for longer than you expect. You should also be working to build up an emergency fund, putting a portion of each paycheck into a savings account to help ensure that you have the cash to cover any lost income in case something does come up. It's a good idea to keep enough money in your emergency fund to cover three to six months of expenses so that you're prepared for the unexpected.

LIFE INSURANCE

Life insurance may also be an important part of your benefits package, especially if you have children and/or you serve as your family's primary breadwinner. Having this kind of coverage helps ensure that your family can continue to handle everyday expenses if you were to pass away. It's especially valuable, because unlike retirement plans, payments from a life insurance plan are tax free upon death. If you were to leave your family $500,000 in a retirement account, taxes would be levied on that money. But with life insurance, the amount of coverage you've been provided by your employer or purchased on your own is what your beneficiaries get.

---

24   "Family and Medical Leave Act," *US Department of Labor Wage and Hour Division*. www.dol.gov/whd/fmla.

Many employers offer group term life insurance. These types of plans cover you while you're employed, or part of the "group." But once you leave, then you're no longer considered a group member, and the corresponding coverage ends. This could create a real problem if you develop a serious condition such as cancer during the time you're employed. Once you leave your job and lose that group coverage, you may be considered "uninsurable" due to your health issues, making it difficult to secure coverage on your own.

If you don't think that group term insurance will work for you in the long run—perhaps you only plan to be with your current employer for a few years, or you want more coverage than your company offers—you can easily purchase your own life insurance plan. It's probably a good idea to have your own coverage in most situations, even if you don't plan to leave your company. You don't want to find yourself out of work and uninsurable years down the line after a layoff or retirement, for instance.

When it comes to life insurance, you have two main options: term insurance and permanent insurance.

TERM INSURANCE

Think of term insurance like an apartment rental. Your plan is almost like a lease, lasting for a certain period of time—usually ten, twenty, or thirty years—and then ends when the term is up. If you save money in other accounts, your children will be grown, your bills will be paid off after that set period of time, and you may find that you won't need life insurance anymore, since you'll have other means of covering your expenses. As such, term plans are a great choice for many families. These plans are often much cheaper and provide a larger amount of coverage than do permanent plans, making them a strong option if your needs fit the criteria mentioned above. Life insurance is cheapest when you're young and healthy, too, so consider locking in those rates early and buying a plan as soon as you have dependents. A quick tip in terms of rates: If you do have some health issues and find yourself paying a higher premium, then you can modify your lifestyle to improve your health, reapply, and potentially get a lower rate.

PERMANENT INSURANCE

The rest of your life insurance options are considered "permanent," since they don't expire after a set period of time, and instead last until your death (as long as you continue to pay your premiums). These plans consist of an insurance portion and an investment portion. The first part goes toward the death benefit—the set amount of money your beneficiaries will receive upon your death, while the second part is invested to create "cash value," money you can access while you're living and borrow against in the form of a loan once it builds up. In some cases, you can even use it to cover the cost of your premiums altogether.[25]

With this two-pronged structure, you also have the option to make changes to your life insurance plan over time. For example, if you were to take out a $250,000 permanent policy when you were thirty years old, and now, at age sixty-five, you've built up significant cash value in your plan—as well as substantial savings in other accounts—then you may determine that you no longer need the full $250,000 in coverage. Instead, you may choose to lower your coverage to $150,000 and use the cash value in the account to cover your premiums going forward.

There are a few types of plans that fall under the umbrella of

---

25   "Whole Life Insurance," *Investopedia*, April 5, 2018, www.investopedia.com/terms/w/wholelife.asp.

permanent life insurance. While all of them consist of insurance and investment portions, there are slight differences. Here are your options and a bit about how they differ:

- *Whole Life*: With whole life insurance, you pay a fixed premium for a set period of time for a lifetime of coverage and get the same cash-value benefits mentioned above. While it's not guaranteed, you also have the opportunity to receive dividends from the investment portion of your plan, which can be applied toward your premiums or toward the purchase of additional coverage.[26]

- *Universal Life*: Universal life insurance policies are another, more flexible option. You can adjust your premium payments and the corresponding death benefit your beneficiaries will receive over the course of the plan. As with all permanent life insurance, if the investment portion of your payments grows enough, it can eventually cover the cost of your premiums, eliminating your monthly payments.[27]

- *Variable Life*: Variable life insurance provides yet another option. The major difference between this and other permanent plans is that, within this type of policy there are different types of investments—similar to a mutual fund. That means there is more risk involved, as well as the potential for more rewards, since the cash value can either grow or decrease substantially over time.[28]

---

26 Pooja Dave, "Permanent Life Policies: Whole Versus Universal," *Investopedia*, December 4, 2018, www.investopedia.com/articles/pf/07/whole_universal.asp

27 Mila Araujo, "Universal Life Insurance and How to Know If It's the Choice for You," *The Balance*, May 8, 2018. www.thebalance.com/what-you-need-to-know-about-universal-life-insurance-2645831

28 "Is Variable Life Insurance Worth It?" *PolicyGenius*, www.policygenius.com/life-insurance/is-variable-life-insurance-worth-it.

When choosing life insurance, there is no right or wrong answer; while term insurance is probably the way to go if you're looking for an affordable plan that will meet your family's needs until you can save enough through other vehicles and/or your children can support themselves, a permanent plan might be a good idea if you are looking to diversify your investment portfolio and have already maxed out your savings through other retirement plans, which usually offer better rates. Since permanent life insurance expenses are usually high and the details associated with them can be complicated, it's worth consulting an advisor if you're considering purchasing one.[29]

No matter what type of life insurance you choose, you should have enough of it to replace your earnings long term if you were to pass away, making it a good idea to have about ten times your income in coverage.

PENSION PLANS

While pensions used to be far more common than they are today, many public-sector organizations still offer them. Employers contribute toward pension plans for the benefit of their employees, and those funds are invested to generate earnings that provide support to employees after they retire.[30]

There are two types of pension plans: defined contribution plans and defined benefit plans.

---

29 "When Is Whole Life Insurance a Good Investment Strategy?" *Nerd-Wallet*, November 13, 2018. www.nerdwallet.com/blog/insurance/whole-life-insurance-good-investment-strategy/

30 "What Is a Pension Plan?" *Investopedia*, June 28, 2018. www.investopedia.com/terms/p/pensionplan.asp

DEFINED CONTRIBUTION PLANS

With a defined contribution plan, employees have the opportunity to contribute to their plans, and employers match those contributions. Anything you contribute is always yours to keep, but you may have to wait a number of years until the match provided by your employer is "fully vested," at which point you actually receive all of the money your employer has added to the pot. After retirement, you'll receive regular payments that eventually total the amount contained in your account, though the total benefit depends on how well the plan's investments perform.[31]

DEFINED BENEFIT PLANS

In a defined benefit plan, employees are guaranteed to receive a certain percentage of their income after retirement, usually based on their earnings and the amount of time spent at the organization. If you find that your company offers a defined benefit plan, it's important to know how long you'll have to be there to get your pension, the percentage of your salary that you'll receive after staying with the organization for the specified period of time, and any other parameters involved. As we saw with Terry in Chapter 2, vesting comes into play here, too. You'll want to know when you're eligible to reap the maximum benefit, and keep that in mind if you ever consider leaving the company—especially if you've been there for a long time.[32]

---

31   Ibid.

32   "What Is a Pension Plan?" *Investopedia*; "Pension Law: An Overview," *Legal Information Institute*. www.law.cornell.edu/wex/pension#

401(K)S

If your organization doesn't offer a pension plan for retirement savings, it may provide a 401(k) instead, an employee-funded plan that allows you to make contributions on a pre- or post-tax basis. You choose the percentage of your paycheck you want to contribute each month, and the money is invested and grows on a tax-deferred basis. Since your contributions are percentage based, if you get a raise, that growth will be captured by your account, too, and you'll end up investing more—making saving for retirement even easier.

GET THE MOST OUT OF YOUR MATCH

You should also find out if your company will match a certain portion of your contributions, since this is essentially free money. Make sure you're contributing as much as your employer will match to get as much free money as possible. For example, if you find that your employer will match up to 6 percent of your salary, then you, too, should be putting in that 6 percent.

DETERMINE YOUR VESTING PERIOD

The next piece to figure out is how long you have to be there to be fully vested, and receive all of the money your employer contributed to your account while you were there. As with pension plans, you can always take your contribution with you when you go, but you may have to work there for several years to get everything your employer has invested on your behalf.[33] If you'll be fully vested after five years, and you've been at your company for three, it might be worth it to

---

33 Miriam Caldwell, "What Does It Mean to Be Vested in My 401(k)?" *The Balance*, October 30, 2018. www.thebalance.com/ what-does-it-mean-to-be-vested-in-my-401-k-2385773

stick it out for the next two years to get the full match—even if you're unhappy.

CHOOSE YOUR INVESTMENTS WISELY

Soon after your job starts, you'll receive a packet in the mail with a full explanation of how your 401(k) works. As you read through the materials, you'll find that you can choose how to invest the money in your account—and you usually have around twenty different options. Imagine going to the grocery store and selecting ingredients to create a satisfying meal. Similarly, this is your opportunity to pick the products that will create a fulfilling spread. No one wants to eat a meal only of rice, corn, potatoes, and pasta, and you should avoid making a similar mistake here.

NO ONE WANTS TO EAT A MEAL ONLY OF RICE, CORN, POTATOES, AND PASTA, AND YOU SHOULD AVOID MAKING A SIMILAR MISTAKE HERE.

It's crucial to diversify, taking into account your age, your risk tolerance, and a number of other factors that can help dictate your choices. But don't just set it and forget it. You'll likely need to adjust your investments based on the inevitable changes that will arise over the course of your life.

Most of the people who come to me for help navigating their 401(k) don't even realize they have options, because those who don't choose their investments are just enrolled in a standard plan. I've had clients come in with 401(k) plans they've had for years—accounts that had accrued hundreds of thousands of dollars. However, the funds were sitting in money market accounts, earning very little interest, since the clients didn't know what they had opted into many years ago. If they had known they had options, and taken the time to choose their investments early on, they could have earned much more money in those accounts over the course of their careers. With one small tweak, placing their funds in a diversified portfolio rather than a low-interest savings account, and subsequent monitoring to make sure their money was performing as best as it could, I was able to help them get a much higher return.

GET HELP WHEN THINGS GET CONFUSING

The ins and outs of retirement accounts can be overwhelming—that's one of the many reasons financial advisors exist in the first place. Even when people do realize they have the opportunity to make investment selections, they're usually not sure how to pick the ones that align with their goals and objectives. They know they have plans filled with "ingredients" to choose from, but they're not sure what those ingredients are—let alone how to create a balanced meal. If you're navigating a 401(k) for the first time, I recommend reaching out to someone you trust who has experience in this area, or finding a financial professional to help you sort through your options based on your individual circumstances. It's also worth it to take a look at your 401(k) once a year—with an expert or on your own—and see how your money is performing and whether you're nearing your goals. Then you can make adjustments as needed.

Another thing to be aware of: Through these plans, you can often get company stock at a discount. While purchasing company stock at a low price may seem like a great deal, especially if you're working for an established organization, be careful about buying too much. If all of your money is invested in one place, and the company drops significantly in value or even fails entirely, all of your hard-earned cash goes down with it.

If you don't want to do a lot of choosing or monitoring, many plans offer what are called "lifetime funds" or "lifecycle funds"—diversified portfolios that adjust as you age. These accounts move your money from more aggressive investments to more conservative ones as you age. If you start saving at age twenty-six, the fund will adapt over time, slowly changing the mixture of investments in your portfolio so that, by the time you reach retirement age, your money has done most of its growing and has been moved to low-risk investments, making it ready for withdrawal when you are.

If you don't take advantage of your company's retirement savings plans, then you're definitely losing out. Take Brian's case, which is common—and unfortunate. When Brian arrived at my office, he was only four years into his career, but his lack of action had cost him thousands. He had chosen not to participate in his employer's 401(k) plan, thinking he'd only be at his company for a short time. Plus, he was young, and he wanted more cash to play with each month. But in the process, he'd missed out on saving—and growing—a significant amount of money for his future, as well as on his employer's match. If he had put away just 5 percent of his salary over four years, he would have contributed $12,000 toward retirement, which would have been matched entirely by his employer, for a total of $24,000.

BUILDING YOUR OWN RETIREMENT PLAN? HERE'S WHAT YOU NEED TO KNOW

Not all companies offer a retirement savings plan like a 401(k), especially smaller companies. If you get a job offer and learn that the company doesn't have one, you may want to consider a different employer or put your own retirement plan in place to make sure you're saving for your future. For example, you have the option of purchasing an individual retirement account, or IRA, on your own. The two most common types are traditional and Roth IRAs.

- *Traditional IRAs*: As long as you're younger than age 70.5 and bring in taxable income, you can contribute to a traditional IRA. And if you don't have a retirement plan at work, you can usually deduct all of your contributions to this account from your tax return, lowering your tax bill. The money in your account grows tax deferred until you withdraw it, typically when you retire, at which point you pay taxes on the money you take out.[34] You can withdraw money from your account at any time, but if you're under age 59.5, you'll have to pay an additional 10 percent penalty on anything you take out, in addition to any taxes owed on that money in the year received.[35]

- *Roth IRAs*: You can contribute to a Roth account at any age, as long as you make less than a certain amount of money per year (check with the IRS to determine the current income cap). While your contributions aren't tax deductible, you don't have to pay tax on withdrawals, although the same 10 percent penalty applies if you withdraw before age 59.5. If you're younger, a Roth IRA might be the better option for you, since you'll pay taxes on that money before you put it in, but it will be tax free to pull it out. At that point, you'll probably be in a higher tax bracket—meaning you'll pay less taxes on that money overall.

---

34 "What Is an IRA?" *Fidelity Investments*. www.fidelity.com/building-savings/learn-about-iras/what-is-an-ira; "Traditional and Roth IRAs," *Internal Revenue Service*. www.irs.gov/retirement-plans/traditional-and-roth-iras.

35 Ibid.

While building a thorough understanding of your benefits package is a crucial part of getting on board at a new job, in this day and age it's hard to rely exclusively on an employer to meet all of your needs. Companies and their policies are changing faster than ever, and their policies change with them. You've likely seen your cell phone provider, Internet company, or bank change hands or practices multiple times over the course of your relationship with them, and jobs are no different. Maintaining a take-care-of-yourself-type mentality is worthwhile in our current climate, especially since people rarely stay in the same position for the duration of their career.

You can and should take advantage of any benefits offered to you, like health insurance, or a 401(k) plan with an employer match, but don't hesitate to put your own plans in place, if you can afford it. For example, you could contribute the minimum amount to get an employer match in your company's 401(k)—say it's 5 percent—and *then* put another 5 percent into a Roth IRA. There are multiple reasons why this is a good idea. You're creating diversification with tax-free and/or tax-deductible money, and if you change or lose your job, then you have an alternative retirement plan already in place that you can continue saving into.

Ask your employer if they offer a Roth 401(k). If so, take full advantage while you are younger and need the tax write-off. And if you want to put in more than the maximum, a standard Roth IRA is a valuable and convenient option for contributing long term to a tax-free investment.

With a thorough understanding of some of the benefits you may be offered, as well as ways to handle gaps in your coverage, let's cover a few other things—both a tactical and bigger picture—to think about when starting your first job or getting settled in a new role.

BE CAREFUL WITH TAX WITHHOLDINGS

You probably know the old adage, coined by Benjamin Franklin: "In this world nothing can be said to be certain, except death and taxes."[36] This remains true more than two hundred years later. It also applies to your new job, since you'll most certainly be paying taxes on the money you earn. When you start working, you'll be asked to fill out a W-4 form, a document that helps your employer withhold the right amount of federal taxes from your pay. On the form, you have the opportunity to indicate how much money your employer should take out, based on a few factors, including the number of dependents you have.

It's not uncommon for people to find that, because of the selections they've made on the form, they haven't had enough taxes withheld during the year. When tax time comes, they realize they owe more money, and they haven't necessarily saved enough to pay it all. If you don't have a home, children, or a retirement account, then you don't need to include any withholdings on your W-4. Make sure to claim 0 or 1 on the form if you don't want to owe at the end of the year.

If your job offers bonuses, be careful with those, too. Sometimes, taxes aren't withheld from them, so if your bonus is big you may owe much more at the end of the year than you thought you would. And a significant bonus can even push you into a higher tax bracket, requiring you to pay Uncle Sam a larger portion of your salary. Filling out your W-4 form carefully, and making sure to account for bonuses when you consider how much you might owe, can help save you from any unpleasant surprises when tax time rolls around.

Now for some of the bigger-picture stuff, including one factor that influences your finances, even though it may seem unrelated.

---

36   Benjamin Franklin to Jean-Baptiste Leroy, November 1789.

DON'T UNDERESTIMATE THE POWER OF EXPOSURE

Whether we realize it or not, we tend to imitate the behaviors of those around us—the people we spend the most time with. The same goes for your financial life. If you surround yourself with friends who spend their paychecks recklessly, with no plans for retirement, then you'll probably find yourself adopting the same set of behaviors. But if you can find people who take a long-game approach to their lives, delaying gratification to reach their goals, then you're likely to do the same.

Why do I bring this up now? Whether you're reading this chapter as you begin your adult career or are looking for advice as you start a new phase—personal or professional—the behaviors you establish now will have a long-term impact on your life. Be smart about the company you keep, and their collective intelligence is likely to change your perspective and progress for the better.

IT'S NOT WHAT YOU MAKE—IT'S WHAT YOU'RE WORTH

Another key concept goes beyond tax forms and 401(k)s: You don't have to make a lot of money to retire rich. The opposite is also true: we've all seen celebrities and athletes who've made and squandered millions of dollars over the course of their careers. Regardless of appearances—the cars they drive or the clothes they wear—a look at their finances would reveal very little saved and loads of debt. By the same token, I've worked with hundreds of clients, schoolteachers, and public servants who never made close to six figures over the course of their careers. But they were able to retire in their mid-fifties with great lives.

There's a big difference between net worth and income. You can make $50,000 per year and have a net worth of $500,000, while someone making $200,000 may have nothing in the bank. Appearances rarely tell the whole story. We all know people who have lived in the same small house for most of their lives. From the outside, it may not look like they have much, but if you dig a little deeper, you might find that the house is paid up and has grown in value over the years, and they've saved diligently in a retirement plan. Now that they're retired, they have enough saved to live the life they want, travel, invest in their children and grandchildren's education, and leave behind a legacy that makes them proud.

Meanwhile, their neighbors may be renting a beautiful house next door, driving a luxury vehicle, and displaying all the trappings of wealth—without any net worth and mounting fears about how to keep the lights on in their fancy chandelier. If you had to choose one of these paths, which would you pick? If the former sounds like a better option, now is the time to lay the groundwork.

ANYTIME YOU MAKE A DECISION—FINANCIAL OR OTHERWISE—ASK YOURSELF, HOW IS THIS GOING TO AFFECT ME IN TEN WEEKS? IN TEN MONTHS? IN TEN YEARS?

If you're just starting out, the choices you make about how you save and spend money can make all the difference. These are the yearning years—you're just beginning to establish your life, financial and otherwise, and the work you put in now will set you up for a strong and healthy future.

A good rule to keep in mind as you make choices about your spending, saving, and anything else is: ten, ten, ten. Anytime you make a decision—financial or otherwise—ask yourself, how is this going to affect me in ten weeks? In ten months? In ten years? Maybe the answer is "not much, go for it." But if it gives you pause—if you're not sure about taking on an expensive car payment, or quitting your job to follow your dreams without a backup plan in mind, or pulling money out of your retirement account to pay for something you don't really need, then it's time to reevaluate that decision.

RECAPPING THE ESSENTIALS

There's so much to think about when you start a new job, and we've covered a lot, but here's a short list of things to remember when that offer letter comes through:

- *First, figure out your benefits.* Knowing the benefits available to you is essential, so make sure you're familiar with every part of your package, and take steps to find alternatives if your company doesn't offer a product or service you need.

- *Understand the ins and outs of your retirement plan.* Learn everything you can about your retirement plan so that you get the most out of it, including the investment choices available to you (if there are any), whether your employer offers a match, and when you'll be fully vested.

- *It may pay to purchase certain plans and packages on your own, even if your company offers them.* With things like life insurance and retirement savings plans, you may want to purchase your own, even if you have coverage through your employer. You can always keep and control the plans you buy, making any job changes less intimidating.

- *Make sure your organization is withholding enough tax.* Be careful when you fill out that W-4, or if you receive a bonus each year. You want to make sure your company is taking out enough taxes so you don't end up owing money you weren't planning to put up when April comes around.

- *Consider the company you keep.* Surround yourself with people who save and spend smartly, and you'll find yourself adopting similar habits.

- *Know the difference between income and net worth.* It's your net worth that matters, not your income. While you can't always control the latter, thinking about the long-term impact of your choices, being practical with your money, and living below your means will help you keep more in the bank for a better tomorrow.

THE BEGINNING'S EASY IF YOU DO IT RIGHT

The beginning's easy—if you do it right, that is. Once everything is in place, you shouldn't have to do much, other than monitoring the accounts and plans you've selected from time to time to make sure you're on the right track. Right now you're sowing seeds, so that when you're ready to retire and relax after years of work, you'll have a tree with fruit to pick and plenty of shade to sit under.

However, if you keep chopping off the branches, that tree is going suffer. You don't want to find yourself in your seventies and scrounging for shade and fruit. In Chapter 5, we'll cover the next phase in life: settling down. You'll learn how to earn successfully, and tend to that sapling for the most promising future possible.

CHAPTER 5

SETTLING DOWN

When you're ready to settle down, things can get a little more complicated. If you're thinking about making any of the big decisions that typically come with this stage—getting married, purchasing a home, having children, or all three—you're taking on additional responsibilities that will have a significant impact on every aspect of your life, including your finances. As such, it's important to be smart along the way. You're essentially tending the soil, working to nourish your future without depleting your resources in the process. Do it right and you'll be on your way to building strong roots for yourself and those you love most. In this chapter, we'll discuss some of the milestones that come with settling down and setting yourself up for a successful tomorrow. We'll start with a pivotal event in most people's lives: marriage.

BEFORE THOSE WEDDING BELLS RING

It's easy to think about all the positives that come with marriage—ideally spending forever with the love of your life, for one. But there are also a number of financial factors to think about. With the potential for tax breaks, two incomes, and just one home to worry about, people often assume that marriage will make their financial lives better, but sometimes it makes things worse. If your future spouse has significant debt, a mortgage, a vastly different income, or even just a different spending philosophy than you do, then you may find yourself facing some serious hurdles that affect not only your wallet, but also your relationship.

WITH THE POTENTIAL FOR TAX BREAKS, TWO INCOMES, AND JUST ONE HOME TO WORRY ABOUT, PEOPLE OFTEN ASSUME THAT MARRIAGE WILL MAKE THEIR FINANCIAL LIVES BETTER, BUT SOMETIMES IT MAKES THINGS WORSE.

Alex and Beth knew about the potential pitfalls of marriage and money. Both of them had watched their own parents grow up arguing about how to pay the bills, and they didn't want to clash over cash after saying "I do." So, they headed to my office shortly after they got engaged and well in advance of their big day. Alex had some credit card debt—about $11,000—left over from his college days, while Beth did not, and their goal was to work together to pay it off to avoid any issues down the line, once they were ready to buy a house and have children. Their current expenses were pretty low, and with big plans for the future, their bills were only going to go up once they got married and started growing their family. That made it a perfect time to use any extra income they had to reduce Alex's debt. I helped them determine how much they could put toward the balance each month, and build a budget with the goal of bringing the amount he owed down to zero.

To avoid paying any more interest, they transferred the debt to a card offering 0 percent interest for the first eighteen months of usage, allowing them to work on the balance without any additional fees. At the end of our session, I told them that if they stuck to our plan, they'd be done within a year—months before their wedding—and able to sail into marriage without that particular worry weighing on them.

But to get to that point, where they could walk into my office and address their issues, they had to discuss their financial lives—past, current, and future—in detail and agree on a path forward. They both realized they were each taking on a financial partner for the long haul, and accepted all the challenges and benefits that came along with that commitment. And even though Alex had entered into the relationship with debt, the couple had very similar ideas about what they wanted out of life and were willing to save more and spend less to get there. Financially, that's a match made in heaven. Without that kind of alignment, it's a much rougher road.

FIND YOUR FINANCIAL FIT

So many marriage problems stem from conflict over money issues. It's one of the most common challenges I see, and it cuts across all sections of the population: wealthy, poor, older, younger—no one is exempt. I'm no marriage counselor, but I'm sure one would agree that it's crucial to make sure you're on the same page when it comes to how you view money. If you both take a similar approach to your finances, then you're going to have an easier time than a couple in which one person is a spender, planning luxury vacations and leasing top-of-the-line cars, while the other is holed up at home eating peanut-butter-and-jelly sandwiches to save every penny. If you're not a fit financially, then you're bound to fight over some of the key choices you'll have to make as a couple.

Being on the same page can save you a lot of cash long-term, not to mention heartache. To get there, you need to understand ahead of time the lifestyle your future spouse wants to have and whether his or her idea of a comfortable existence aligns with your own. How do you know if you've found someone whose approach to finances will mesh with yours? Ask. Find out what kind of home your spouse wants to live in, inquire about his or her philosophy on driving cars—whether he or she believes a new one every few years is necessary or if he or she'd be happy in something used but sturdy. Discuss whether you both want to have children, and, if you do, whether it makes sense for one of you to stay home with the kids. Figure out how much you should have in an emergency fund based on what your joint income will be, reflect on what you want your retirement to look like, and determine how you can reach those goals together. And if your ideas about your future don't align, then think about whether you can compromise.

Another good indicator of how your partner will behave financially: Take a look at how they were raised. People often imitate the financial habits they grew up around. If your fiancé had parents who lived at or above their means, then he or she is likely to spend similarly. After all, families are the primary models we have. But uncovering information like this probably won't just come up naturally; it usually requires that you inquire about his or her history.

SHARE YOUR FINANCIAL GOALS

At the very least, make sure to talk about your financial goals before you take the next step. I would say that more than half of my clients haven't had this very crucial conversation—especially those getting married for the first time. I get it; this stuff isn't your typical dinner talk. Few people think to ask about their partner's 401(k) over burgers or sushi, even though those retirement savings will certainly matter down the line. I also understand that you want your relationship to be about more than just money. But this isn't the time to be shy. The way you both spend and save will affect everything you do. As such, working toward a unified financial goal affects your whole relationship for the better.

While love is certainly powerful, money has the potential to cause real problems in your marriage and beyond. If you realize your money perspectives aren't perfectly matched, then proceed with caution. It can be easy to regard your significant other's rocky financial past as something that's not a big deal or that will be fixable later on. But habits (and debt) die hard, and you may feel differently when the way he or she handles money has deadly consequences for *your* finances. Not to mention the fact that once you're officially married, you're on the hook for many of those mistakes.

John experienced this firsthand. He and his wife, Sally, had been married for years, but things just weren't working out and they were in the process of getting divorced. Unfortunately, it wasn't only the end of the marriage that John had to deal with. Sally had taken out multiple credit cards in John's name and racked up big balances while they had been married—a few of which he didn't even know about—and she hadn't been paying them down.

Meanwhile, John had been very responsible with his money, never spending more than he had and paying off his credit card bills in full every month. Through his diligence, he had built up a great credit score over the years. But by taking out new cards, spending lavishly, and leaving balances hanging, Sally damaged that score. Since John's credit score would be taken into account when he went to rent or buy a new home or vehicle, or even get a job, Sally's choices would have a real impact on his ability to move forward long after their relationship ended. Worse, he would still be responsible for those lingering bills. While Sally and John had reached the point of irreconcilability, they could have addressed some of their issues earlier on with a tactic that can be hard to come by: honesty.

THE BEST POLICY: HONESTY

Occasionally, a client will call me and share that he's embarrassed to tell his fiancé about his financial situation. He'd rather work with me to fix his problems on his own so that he doesn't have to disclose them to his wife-to-be.

My advice: Be open and honest about your situation. Consider meeting a financial advisor with your fiancé up front, like Beth and Alex did. Even if your financial background isn't the best, most people will be able to appreciate that you're trying to improve the situation. Plus, if you work together to ensure that your finances are in order ahead of your wedding day, you'll build trust—along with a strong plan to move forward as a couple. It'll be one less challenge you'll run into once you're married (and trust me, challenges are inevitable). If you're currently in a tricky situation, or you find yourself in one in the future, be honest about it so that you can take action and avoid a worse outcome later on.

Ted can attest to the value of honesty. He was totally blindsided by a huge problem he didn't see coming: his wife, Jill, hadn't been paying their mortgage. Ted was a stay-at-home dad, taking care of the couple's three children while Jill worked full time. Since Jill was the breadwinner, she typically handled all of the bills. One day, Ted went to check the mail and found an urgent notice from their lender. Months had gone by without a single payment. Late fees had built up, and now they were at risk of foreclosure.

All the while, Jill had been spending big on luxury items: a new high-end car, handbags, expensive clothes for work, and extravagant gifts for their children. Ted had noticed her spending, but he figured she must have been making enough to cover it all. Instead, purchasing expensive things had become something of an addiction for Jill, and she was simply skipping out on the bills she couldn't afford to pay. She kept telling herself she'd just catch up later. When her spending became an overwhelming problem, she didn't tell Ted because she was afraid of how he would react.

Now they had no other option but to deal with the issue together. And they only had a few choices, none of which were good: file bankruptcy, start liquidating their assets, or spend on childcare so that Ted could start working as well to help pay down their debt. Addressing a financial problem like this one is similar to fixing a car when you've never changed the oil: what could have been handled easily and cheaply balloons into a big, expensive issue with no easy out. It was time to make some really tough decisions. They had to figure out what they were going to forgo or sacrifice to pay what they owed, and it would take them years of work and therapy to get back on stable ground, both financially and emotionally. To do it all, they would need to do something they probably should have done much earlier on: seek expert support.

GET EXPERT HELP

Marriage is like a business. If you were taking on a professional partner, then you'd be sure that you shared the same vision, wouldn't you? And if you were brand new to business as a whole, you'd probably seek help too, reaching out to someone who had been there before to get some ideas on how to manage it all. Similarly, when it comes to marriage, don't be afraid to get assistance from a third party. If you suspect that something is up with your partner and don't feel comfortable posing tough-to-ask questions, then find someone who can tactfully ask them on your behalf—whether that's a marriage counselor, a financial advisor, or even a close friend. If your fiancé is reluctant to see someone, it may be a sign that he or she is hiding something. And though the process might be uncomfortable or even painful, it's better to know what you're in for now so that you can take action right away, whether that means creating a plan, paying down any debts, or even heading your separate ways.

I bet Bram and Evelyn wish they had had these kinds of conversations with a professional earlier on. Just a few months ago, they decided to see a financial advisor for the first time after months of arguing. Bram has worked for the city for many years, and he's nearing retirement. He's ready to spend his days fishing, playing golf, and spending time with his grandchildren. He never imagined doing those activities alone, but then again, he and Evelyn hadn't really planned for retirement *together*. Bram never thought it was worth a conversation since his government job had given him a straightforward path throughout his career. He would finish working just before he turned sixty and take a generous pension. It had always seemed as simple as that.

Evelyn, on the other hand, has owned a small flower shop for the past twenty years, and she's about as married to her job as she is to Bram. She leaves the house at 5:30 a.m. each day to shop for wholesale flowers for her store and doesn't return until late in the evening, when the last bouquet has left the building. Evelyn has no desire to retire—her shop is her primary passion, and she can't imagine her life without it. She also hasn't done a lot of saving; she's put much of what she's earned into growing her business. Even if she wanted to stop working, she isn't sure they could afford it. With no resolution in sight, they called me, looking to dissolve their disagreements and figure out what their future could look like.

Bram and Evelyn's ongoing issues demonstrate the importance of having these discussions and getting support out of the gate. If couples spent half the time they took planning their wedding and honeymoon to think about their financial future, there'd probably be far fewer disagreements and divorces. If you're getting ready for marriage—one of the biggest game changers there is—then you have some talking to do. You have to discuss your financial perspectives, the kind of life you want, and how to get there together. That's the way to make it work. And if you can't figure it all out on your own, don't be afraid to ask for help.

THINKING ABOUT BUYING A HOME? READ THIS FIRST

For many of the couples I see, the first goal they set their sights on after marriage is buying a home. Purchasing property is often a good idea—it will help you diversify your finances and give you an asset that will (ideally) appreciate in value over time, putting more money in your pocket if and when you decide to sell. As with any big decision, though, you have to consider your individual circumstances. Purchasing doesn't make sense for everyone. In some areas, buying is extremely expensive, and renting might provide more control and flexibility. Those who are older and don't want to deal with the upkeep on a home, who travel a lot for work, or who plan to move in the near future might find that owning isn't right for them. But if you're a young couple just starting out, it may very well make sense to be paying toward something that's yours to keep and building equity—all while getting a tax deduction.

If you determine that buying a home is the way to go, then you need to figure out what's most important to you. Consider these questions and add your own to the list to help identify what matters most:

- Do you want to get more house for your money and live farther from the nearest city, or would you rather be closer to a metropolitan area and pay more money for less space?

- Do you want something brand new, or would you be happy with a home that has a little history?

- What features are most important to you? A large kitchen to turn out impressive meals? Or is a big living room that can host a crowd for family game nights and holidays the big priority? Perhaps you'd trade indoor space for a big backyard, or even a pool?

- If you're single, are you planning to get married and have kids? And if you are, how are the schools in the area where you're looking?

SET A REASONABLE BUDGET

With an idea of what you want, it's time to figure out what you can afford. How much money do you have saved that could go toward a down payment, and what can you pay toward a mortgage each month? While there's no set-in-stone formula, it can be helpful to keep some numbers in mind when you're creating a budget. Try not to spend more than 25 percent of your income on your house note. Maintenance is a key part of the equation, too, and one people often forget about. But once you buy a home, there's no landlord anymore. You're the one handling it all, whether the toilet seat breaks, the dryer dies, or the roof springs a leak. Keeping a pot of $5,000 to $10,000 to cover any maintenance costs means that you won't have to depend solely on credit cards if something goes wrong, so you should factor that into your savings plan, too.

Jake and Ali recently came by for help with their budgeting strategy. They had a clear goal in mind: they had just gotten married, and they wanted to be in their own place by their second anniversary. They had some wedding money and the support of their families, who were willing to contribute toward the down payment, but it wasn't quite enough to get a place they liked. I sat down with them and took a look at their finances to help them figure out a reasonable budget and timeline.

Together, we determined that, between mortgage rates and other associated expenses, buying a house would cost them about $600 more than their current rental per month—another factor to think about while budgeting. They'd have to spend a little less each month to get there within the next two years, but they were happy to have fewer meals and drinks out if it meant they would have a home to call their own. I also made sure they would be saving enough so that if they had to break their lease—a worthwhile expense if you get a good deal on a place—they could. Eighteen months later, they were holding the keys to their new house.

Saving enough to buy a house doesn't happen overnight. But if you put in the work and plan right, then you'll eventually be able to afford something great.

CONSIDER PMI TO MAKE HOMEOWNERSHIP POSSIBLE

When it comes to buying a home, you have a couple of different options to pay for it. You can either put the standard 20 percent down, or you can pay less and get property mortgage insurance, or PMI, to account for the difference. PMI can make homeownership a little more accessible, especially if you have many expenses and only a little bit saved toward a down payment. With PMI—an extra monthly charge—you can put less than 20 percent down on a home, and the insurance protects your lender in case you default. It usually costs anywhere from .3 percent to 1.5 percent of the total loan annually.[37] There are many different arguments for and against PMI, but my personal perspective is this: Think about how you can get into your new home with the least amount of money down. You don't want to be in a situation where you don't have any cash on hand for emergencies. I've seen people drop their entire life savings on a down payment and then struggle when their car breaks down or they need a new water heater.

Plus, for many young couples, a 20 percent deposit—the typical cost of a down payment without PMI—is pretty unrealistic. If you're looking at a $200,000 house—which would be slightly cheaper than the average cost of a home in the United States at $222,800—that's $40,000 down.[38] Very few of the young people I've worked with in Middle America have that much sitting in a bank account or are

---

37   Dori Zinn, "What Is PMI? Learn the Basics of Private Mortgage Insurance," *Bankrate*, September 11, 2018. www.bankrate.com/finance/mortgages/the-basics-of-private-mortgage-insurance-pmi.aspx.

38   "United States Home Prices and Values," *Zillow*, https://www.zillow.com/home-values.

capable of saving it up in a relatively short period of time. It's also rare that people move into a new home and don't change a thing—you'll probably want to have some cash left over to make modifications. At minimum, you'll want to paint a wall. There's also the cost of moving and movers to think about. And if you're going to stay in a home for a while, then it's probably going to appreciate, meaning it might be worth it to get into a place sooner rather than later and build some equity along the way. The bottom line: When you buy a home, try to keep as much cash in your pocket as you can. If that requires getting property mortgage insurance, then it's probably the right choice.

Let's say, for instance, that you have your heart set on a house that's $200,000. If you have 10 percent saved, or $20,000, you could borrow the additional $180,000 necessary to buy the home and get PMI insurance. If the PMI costs you .5 percent of the loan per year, you'd end up paying an additional $90 per month—not a huge expense when you consider all the benefits of homeownership or the time it would take you to save another $20,000—and be able to buy today. You also don't have to keep paying PMI forever; you can always refinance and drop the insurance once you have a little equity in the house.

CHOOSE A MORTGAGE THAT MAKES SENSE

Once you've set a budget and thought about how you'll pay for your home, you can consider your options for a mortgage. When it comes to mortgages, you have two primary choices: fixed-rate and adjustable-rate mortgages. With fixed mortgages, you lock in the interest rate you'll pay for the life of the loan. If you get in at 4 percent interest, it stays at 4 percent for the duration. Adjustable mortgages fluctuate. Every so often, the rate changes—often increasing. However, they can appear more appealing at first, since rates are usually lower to begin with.

Unless you're pretty savvy and you're not planning to be in your home for a long time, going fixed is probably the right choice. What happens if we have another financial crisis, and your mortgage goes up while your home value drops? No one wants to be paying on a $200,000 mortgage for a house that's only valued at $130,000— especially when the interest rate goes up. If you have an adjustable mortgage and a job loss or change leaves you with a lower income, then you'll have to find a way to pay more while making less. That means if you choose an adjustable-rate mortgage, you better know what you're doing—and be aware of how long you're going to stay in your current home, how much interest rates can fluctuate (some adjustable-rate mortgages have caps as to how high or low interest rates can go), as well as what your lifestyle will most likely look like in the years to come.[39]

Janelle and Warren quickly learned this lesson while thinking about their path to homeownership. Before they moved forward, they wanted to double check on whether they were making the right choice, so they made an appointment with me to talk about their plans. They had seen a $300,000 house they loved, and though it was a bit more than their original budget, they had been offered an adjustable-rate mortgage at $2,200 per month, which they could swing. "That's great," I told them. "But what happens in five years when the mortgage adjusts and that $2,200 becomes $2,900 per month? Are you prepared for that?"

---

39 "What is the Difference Between a Fixed-Rate and Adjustable-Rate Mortgage?" *Consumer Financial Protection Bureau*, September 25, 2017, www.consumerfinance.gov/ask-cfpb/what-is-the-difference-between-a-fixed-rate-and-adjustable-rate-mortgage-arm-loan-en-100.

"No, not really," Janelle said. "We'll hopefully have a baby by then, and I'm going to stop working when we do." If they had gone with the $2,200 adjustable-rate mortgage, then they wouldn't have been able to handle the additional cost when their household income and expenses changed significantly. With the understanding that they couldn't account for future interest rates with an adjustable-rate mortgage, they found a home that fit their budget and a fixed mortgage that would stay steady. This is just one example of why it's so important to think about every financial factor in your life when you're considering buying a home—not just today, but tomorrow, too.

The next piece: choosing the length of your mortgage. You usually have ten-, fifteen-, twenty-, or thirty-year options. If you wanted the lowest rate per month, then you'd go with a thirty-year mortgage. A fifteen-year mortgage will create higher monthly payment, but you'll pay it off in half the time. If paying it off more quickly appeals, but you're overwhelmed by the higher payment amount, you could always do a thirty-year mortgage and put little extra toward the principal each month, thus shortening the life of the mortgage and giving yourself the flexibility to pay more when you can, as opposed to being locked into a bigger bill.

Homeownership may seem like a distant dream, but with some careful considerations, a little saving, and a lot of research, it can become your reality faster than you might think. Get clear on what you want in a home, weigh all of the options available to you, and build a budget with current and future expenses in mind, and you'll be on your way to owning a place before you know it.

ENSURE YOUR WALLET'S READY FOR KIDS

Once you're married and living comfortably in your own home, children may be the next logical step. If that's the case, you have to make sure you're prepared financially for that, too. From birth to age seventeen, kids cost families an average of $233,610 *each*—and that's before college is factored in.[40] That's why readying your wallet should be just as big a part of preparing for a new addition as decorating the nursery. Spending less and saving more while you still can is necessary, but you also need to think about their futures in addition to your own.

ACCOUNT FOR THE ADDED COST OF CHILDCARE

One of the biggest choices couples grapple with is whether one spouse should stay home to take care of children once they arrive. Going from two incomes to one is doable in many cases, but it's a big decision that requires careful planning. If you know that you want one parent to be the primary caregiver for your children once they're born, put the work in now. Keep your household expenses low and ensure that you can cover them with just one set of earnings. That may mean purchasing a smaller home or buying used vehicles that you can easily pay off before your children arrive so that payments stay low. You should also make sure that you're both saving as much as you can toward retirement to establish ample funds that will continue to grow. That way, if one of you decides to leave the workforce for a bit, your money will continue to work for you. Think back to Chapter 3, when Michelle began saving for retirement early

---

40   M. Lino et al., "Expenditures on Children by Families, 2015," *US Department of Agriculture*, Center For Nutrition Policy and Promotion, No. 1528-2015, www.cnpp.usda.gov/sites/default/files/crc2015_March2017.pdf.

so that she could fund her future in full *and* stay home with her children when they were little.

While childcare may be a lower-cost option, it's a significant investment as well. Though rates vary significantly by location, most families spend more than 10 percent of their income on childcare and a recent study found that, in twenty-three states, childcare was more expensive than public university tuition.[41] If you and your spouse both plan to work after you have children, make sure your bank account can manage that additional expense.

PROTECT YOUR FAMILY

You should also ensure that you have systems in place to protect your growing family if something should happen to you. If you don't have life insurance, or you have a nominal amount of coverage through work, now is the time purchase it on your own. You should have enough to cover your expenses long-term if you were to pass away—usually about ten times your income. Even if you'll be staying at home rather than bringing in a paycheck, you still need enough coverage to outsource the tasks you would otherwise take care of yourself, such as childcare and cleaning. For more information on life insurance and your options for coverage, check out Chapter 4.

SAVE FOR THEIR FUTURE

Saving for college is also important to many parents, and handling the high cost of tuition means—you guessed it—starting as soon as

---

41 Kerri Anne Renzulli, "This Is How Much the Average American Spends on Child Care," *Money*, August 9, 2016, http://time.com/money/4444034/average-cost-child-care; Ethan Wolff-Mann, "Is Your State One of the 23 Where Pre-K Costs More Than College?" *Money*, April 11, 2016, http://time.com/money/4289032/pre-k-costs-more-than-college-in-23-states.

you can. A 529 plan is a great option for many families, and offers two different programs, depending on whether you think your child will attend a public institution in your state or pursue their education elsewhere. These plans can even be used toward private school tuition, an added benefit if you're thinking about enrolling your child in an alternative school system. Mutual funds provide another opportunity to save if you want fewer restrictions on how you can spend your investment. To learn more about the ins and outs of affording an education, return to Chapter 3.

A SUCCESSFUL LIFE STARTS WITH A PLAN

Settling down and potentially starting a life with someone else is certainly something to celebrate, but it will be a lot more joyful if you do it right. Below are some things to keep in mind, depending on your current priorities.

If you're getting married:

- See if your financial priorities align. If your perspectives align when it comes to money, you'll probably face fewer struggles throughout your relationship. Finances are behind so many of the challenges that arise in a marriage, and if you're both on the same page, then you'll be a lot better off.

- Talk about the future. Even if you're not perfectly in sync when it comes to money matters, discussing your financial future is extremely important, helping you to avoid disagreements and work toward goals together.

- Be honest. Be honest about any issues that come up. It's much better to tackle them when they first arise—as a team—than to wait until things become overwhelming.

- Get outside support. There's no shame in seeking outside support. Reach out to a financial advisor to ensure that you're on the right path or talk to a counselor when things get rocky. We all need a little help sometimes, and there's no substitute for expert advice.

If you're thinking about buying a home:

- *Discuss what you want in a home.* Determine the characteristics that matter most to you—ranking space, layout, location, nearby school systems, and any other qualities you care about. Use those items to evaluate any properties that you're considering.

- *Build a budget.* Look at your current savings and expenses and think about what you can afford, taking into account that you don't want to deplete your savings entirely, and that home expenses should ideally take up 25 percent or less of your household income.

- *Consider PMI.* If a 20 percent down payment is out of reach, property mortgage insurance may be the way to go. Paying a small percentage of your loan each year can allow you to get into a house with less down, making homeownership accessible for younger couples and anyone with less cash saved.

- *Choose the right type of mortgage.* Adjustable-rate mortgages—in which rates fluctuate on a set schedule—might seem more appealing because of their low introductory rates, but in most cases, fixed-rate mortgages, which offer the same interest rate for the life of the loan, are the way to go. You should also think about how much time you want to spend paying off your loan. While mortgages with shorter terms cost more per month, they'll be paid off faster and accrue less interest over time.

If you're thinking about children:

- *Determine your plans for childcare.* Whether one of you plans to stay home or you'll be outsourcing care to a center or a nanny, budget this significant expense into your current spending and saving efforts before your baby is born.

- *Review your accounts.* This is also a good time to review your investments and any other financial plans you have in place, and make sure they're set up to weather any changes to your living situation or your lifestyle.

- *Make sure your life insurance plan is up to speed.* If you're having kids, add them as beneficiaries under your current life insurance policy. And if you don't have life insurance yet—or you only have a small plan through work—get it now. For more information, check out Chapter 3.

- *Save for college.* If you have a little one on the way, now's the time to think about saving for college. Consider saving in a 529 plan or mutual fund to give your money time to grow so it can handle the ever-rising costs of higher education.

The secret to long-term success is understanding what you're getting into in all circumstances, and prepare your wallet for the impact of any decisions you might make.

When you make a plan, many things are possible—and it's a lot more likely that you'll be able to have more of what you want in life. A plan can serve as your GPS, making sure you're headed in the right direction once you hit the road. If you choose not to use it and just drive in the dark, good luck. It's unlikely that you're going to get where you want to go. But if you put in the thought today, you're almost guaranteed to live a better tomorrow. That means planning for the unexpected, too, since none of us can predict the future. In the next chapter, we'll talk about how to ready yourself for the surprises that are just a part of life.

CHAPTER 6

WEATHERING UNEXPECTED EVENTS

E veryone has had life throw them a curveball at one point or another. Running the gamut from slightly annoying to completely catastrophic, these challenges can catch us off guard in so many ways. I'm no stranger to the unexpected. Just recently, the water main under my yard broke, and my lawn quickly became a swamp. When I called the city to ask what they could do about it, I found that the damage was just a few inches away from what they considered to be "public" territory. I was responsible for the problem. I had to call the plumber and pay to get it fixed. The month before, I had to call a carpenter to repair my deck because of a problem I didn't anticipate, and I'm sure it won't be long before my washer and dryer go south. Most of my friends and colleagues are managing similarly unexpected issues—covering medical expenses for their aging parents who just don't have the means to take care of themselves on their own, or footing the bill for their adult children who are struggling to make ends meet. The older you get, the more you realize that dealing with stuff like this is just adulthood in action.

Life happens, as they say. Cars break down, people get sick, homes and appliances need fixing. You can't avoid the unexpected, but you can plan for it. With smart financial practices in place, you'll make sure that you and your family can cope with the inevitable unknowns that will come your way. In this chapter, we'll highlight a few ways to prepare for the worst, and discuss what happens when you don't.

SAVE FOR A RAINY DAY

Miranda called me to tell me the bad news. She had to have a medical procedure in the near future, and her insurance wasn't going to pay for it. Like many Americans, she was unaware of the details of her insurance, including her deductible and the services her plan did or didn't cover. She was surprised that after the relatively simple but necessary procedure, she'd have to pay thousands of dollars out of pocket. Worse, she didn't have any money stashed away other than what she had saved in her retirement fund. As a result, what started out as a small nuisance was quickly turning into a crisis. The cost of the procedure would cut into what she typically set aside to pay for her other bills. So, as she desperately tried to save—putting aside everything she could—she had fallen behind on her regular expenses. With just a few weeks to go before her appointment, she would have to take a loan on her retirement fund to cover the additional charges and catch up on her missed payments.

While there wasn't much I could do to help her manage her

current issue, I advised that as soon as she paid what she owed, she should start to build up an emergency fund. That way, she'd have extra money that she could pull from when something else popped up. If anything like this were to happen again, she could also take out a credit card that offered zero or low interest on charges for the first twelve to eighteen months. She could then depend on the card to help front anything her account couldn't handle and avoid borrowing on her retirement—especially as she got older and had less time to replace those funds before she stopped working. Miranda's situation illustrates a point that applies to almost any unexpected scenario: If you don't do your homework up front, you end up behind.

Think of planning for an emergency like packing for a vacation. If you don't bring the proper clothing for the climate, then you're going to end up having to rush out and buy something new—often at a higher price than you'd pay otherwise. I've worked with so many people who are caught by surprise by one emergency or another, and because they haven't prepared, they have to give something up. Sometimes, it's saving less toward their retirement to pay more for current expenses. Other times, it's sacrificing time

IF YOU DON'T DO YOUR HOMEWORK UP FRONT, YOU END UP BEHIND.

to create another income stream in the form of a second job, or cutting back significantly on the things they enjoy to make up for unanticipated bills. Plan for the rainy days, because they're going to come at some point.

Trina was quite familiar with rainy days. She had a tough childhood, watching her parents struggle constantly to make ends meet and worry about how to keep the lights on and put food on the table. When she began her own working life, she decided she didn't want her own family to experience anything like what she had been through. She was committed to saving as much as she could, and lived below her means for her entire career and into retirement. When an emergency did arise, she was well prepared.

Recently, her car broke down, and after taking it into her local mechanic, she learned that the problem was pretty much unfixable. It would cost more to get her current vehicle into working order than to buy a new one. Luckily, the car was completely paid off, as was her home. On top of that, she had built up a comfortable retirement and saved an additional $100,000 in the bank over time to deal with events just like this one. Because of her prudence, Trina had more than enough money to buy a great car and pay cash for it.

How did she do it? She realized that she wanted a lush, fruitful tree later in life, so she committed to setting aside much of her earnings early. Every time she paid something off, she diligently contributed the amount she had been paying monthly toward her savings. The same went for raises. Any increase in income went right into her account. Even though tough situations had popped up now and again throughout her life, she had been able to handle them and bounce back.

Since Trina had done such a great job of saving, our next step— once she bought a new car—was to make her money work better for her. She was getting very little interest on the cash she had saved in the bank, so we redistributed it, investing in few different areas, so that she could earn more. And with her mortgage and car taken care of, she could keep adding about half of the distributions she received from Social Security and her retirement fund right back into her savings account.

Had she not done these things, her car breaking down could have been a real crisis. With no money to put down and bad credit, she would have ended up with a bigger car payment and higher interest—which she probably wouldn't have been able to afford on a fixed income. Instead, Trina's doing better than ever. She's finally earning on all those savings, thanks to a diversified portfolio, and spending a bit more on herself. She recently took a vacation to Hawaii, something she's been dreaming about since she was a kid, and was delighted to be able to set up a college fund for her granddaughter. Trina's commitment to saving for a rainy day meant she could create the life she wanted and even invest in her family's future.

Saving for emergencies in a fund separate from retirement and other accounts is also key here. Frequently, people have all their money tied up in a single savings or retirement fund—similar to Miranda's situation. But different types of accounts serve different purposes, and it's important to avoid a situation where you're pulling everything from one place. Not all of your clothes are for winter, right? And if they were, it would make for a pretty uncomfortable July in lots of places. Setting up separate accounts is all part of being prepared for any kind of weather throughout the seasons of your life.

MAKE SURE YOU'RE COVERED—NO MATTER WHAT

Sometimes, a lack of planning can make a very sad situation far more devastating. Lydia experienced this firsthand when the unthinkable happened: her husband was killed in a car accident. Both Lydia and her husband, Tom, worked full time and contributed equally to the household. They were both healthy and had a comfortable middle-class existence. But when Tom died without any warning, Lydia found herself facing two burdens at once—the pain of losing a spouse and the weight of shouldering their family's finances herself.

Tom didn't have life insurance, so Lydia had to figure out what to do to get by without him, both personally and financially. Because she couldn't cover their mortgage on her own, Lydia and her three boys ended up moving in with her parents. Lydia was lucky to have the support of her family. Without their help, she would've found herself facing a real financial struggle in addition to her grief.

When she came to me to begin rebuilding her life, the first thing I told her to do was to take out a significant life insurance plan. Now that she was a single parent, she had to make sure that her children were protected financially. While she was bringing in that sole income—and her kids were depending on it—she would need to have enough life insurance to replace her earnings in full for the sake of her children if she were to die as well.

Lydia's situation is the kind of thing no one wants to think about, but when you avoid it entirely rather than putting systems in place to get through it, you can end up causing yourself more pain. I always ask people, "If you had a machine in your house that gave you $65,000 per year, would you have it insured, so that you'd keep getting that money if it broke or someone stole it?" Of course, you would. That's essentially what life insurance does. It provides your loved ones with those vital funds when you can't. You have to prepare for two potential outcomes: living too long, or dying too soon. Life insurance guards against the latter.

If one spouse works and the other stays at home, it's essential that both partners have coverage. Even if you're not earning an income, all of the work you are doing to help maintain your family's day-to-day lives is going to need to be taken care of—and potentially outsourced—if, God forbid, something happens to you. I've never delivered a death benefit to someone and heard him or her say that it was just too much money. Getting covered helps protect your loved ones. It's a win-win. For more information on life insurance and getting the kind of coverage you need, check out Chapter 4.

BEGIN WITH A BUDGET

The first step in planning for the worst is creating a budget. Making more than you spend is an essential part of saving for an emergency—or anything else. Without a budget, it's hard to know where your money's going. Use the worksheet on page 96 to help build a sensible budget that will allow you to store up the additional funds you need. With this simple tool, you'll be able to clearly see where your money's going and where you can cut back if you find that you're spending too much. Maybe it's making coffee at home instead of hitting up the fancy shop on the way into work, or eating fewer meals out and putting more money in your emergency account each month. No matter how you decide to prepare for the future, you'll be glad you did. And if you make sure to start budgeting before something difficult happens, you'll probably find that the whole process is easier than you thought it would be.

SYSTEMS AND STRATEGIES TO WEATHER THE WORST

No one wants to think about the hard stuff—especially when it comes as a surprise—but doing all you can to safeguard yourself and your family financially will make the toughest times easier. The following systems and strategies can help you weather the worst:

Monthly Income (after taxes)

Income / Salary from all sources	
Investment Income	
Dividends, Interest, Capital Gains	
Other Income	
Total Monthly Income	

Monthly Savings

General (Inc. Emergency Fund)	
College / Other Education	
Retirement	
Other (i.e. House)	
Total Monthly Savings	

Monthly Expenses

HOME	
Mortgage / rent / HOA	
Housecleaning / landscaping	
Electric / Gas	
Water / trash / recycling	
Phone / Internet	
Security	
Total Home	

Personal	
Clothes	
Dry cleaning / laundry	
Barbershop / salon	
Hobbies	
Charitable Donations	
Child care	
Pets	
Total Personal	

Debt Category	
Credit cards	
Other loans / lines	
Total Other	

Education	
Tuition	
Books	
Student loans	
Total Education	

Total Monthly Expenses	

FOOD	
Groceries	
Dining / Takeout	
Total Food	

Health	
Toiletries	
Cosmetics	
Pharmacy	
Health Club	
Medical / Dental	
Total Health	

Entertainment	
Movies / Shows	
Vacation	
Parties / Gifts	
Subscriptions	
Memberships	
Total Entertainment	

Auto / Transport	
Car loan / lease	
Car Insurance	
Maintenance	
Public Transit	
Parking	
Gasoline	
Total Auto	

Total Monthly Income	
- Total monthly expenses	
= Net Cash Flow	

- *Save for a rainy day.* Emergency funds are so important, helping you stockpile cash that can be used toward anything you might need, like medical expenses and car and home repairs. While building up your account balance might take some discipline, when an unexpected expense comes up you'll definitely be glad you did it.

- *Have a no-interest or low-interest credit card on hand.* Having a no-interest or low-interest credit card on hand for additional financial coverage is smart, too. It's not always realistic to have tens of thousands saved in an emergency account, especially if you're just starting to put money away. With a no-or low-interest card, you can rest easy knowing that if you do have to pay for something big, you have the ability to do so—and the time to pay it off with little or no penalty.

- *Ensure you have proper insurance.* Life insurance ensures that if the worst happens, you don't leave your family in a terrible predicament. Getting the right amount of coverage is one of the best things you can do for your loved ones, providing the funds to take care of them if something should happen to you.

- *Don't be afraid to ask for help.* Sometimes, we get into challenging situations. If you have family or friends who might be willing to lend a hand, like in Lydia's situation, it's probably worth it to ask. So many people are too embarrassed to let their community know when they need help, but if those closest to you can lend a hand and help you to avoid interest and late fees to boot, it's often worth the momentary discomfort. For example, I'd rather loan my children money if they needed it and have them pay me back than see them open a credit card with a high interest rate and struggle with the growing balance. Your family members might feel the same, and it could save you a lot of money and grief in the long run.

- *Start young.* The best thing you can do is to start guarding yourself early. It'll be much easier to establish savings, purchase life insurance, and put any other stopgaps into place if you start as soon as possible. There's really no substitute for good planning, and that begins right out of the gate. A budget is a good place to start.

In a sense, the planning we do in financial services is very similar to the medical profession. If you see a doctor before you get sick or as soon as symptoms start, he or she can usually help you avoid serious issues such as diabetes, a heart attack, or stroke, saving you significant pain, stress, money, and more. Similarly, financial advisors can provide preventive care, providing the tools to create healthier, happier lives and an easier recovery when things do go wrong. While it's probably a good idea to seek help from an advisor if something serious happens, you can put some of these protections in place for yourself. It's easy to get started with the tips we've talked about in this chapter: Make sure you're saving in an emergency fund, purchase a life insurance plan if you haven't already so you can continue supporting your family even after you're gone, and practice healthy money habits from now on to get a head start on handling anything that might come your way. I promise you'll be grateful you did.

Next up, we'll cover how to navigate a different kind of shift: mid-career changes.

CHAPTER 7

MAKING MID-CAREER CHANGES

t's not unusual to change course after spending some time in the working world. Knowing exactly what will make you happy when you're just starting out is a rarity, so it shouldn't come as a surprise if you end up interested in something new while you're waist deep in your current career. If you do, you're not alone. In Chapter 4, we talked about how, on average, Americans stay at a particular job for only four-and-a-half years. And it's not just millennials who are constantly switching it up. According to the Bureau of Labor Statistics, on average, baby boomers born between 1957 and 1964 took on nearly twelve different roles between the ages of eighteen and forty-eight.[42] Since most of us will make at least a few career moves

---

42   Domingo Angeles, "Younger Baby Boomers and Number of Jobs Held," *US Department of Labor Bureau of Labor Statistics*, June 2016, www.bls.gov/career-outlook/2016/data-on-display/younger-baby-boomers-and-number-of-jobs-held.htm

throughout our lives, it's helpful to know when to try a new path or stay the course, as well as the financial impact of either decision. Of course, happiness is an essential part of the equation, but determining your next step responsibly requires thorough evaluation—especially if others are depending on you.

There are also some midlife changes that don't necessarily have to do with your career, but still affect your bottom line. These, too, can throw you for a loop. But, as we established in the previous chapters, if your finances are ready for anything, you will be, too. Let's start with a series of things to think about when you're considering a career switch well into adulthood.

LOOK BEFORE YOU LEAP

When the potential to pursue something new arises, many people fail to recognize what they already have. They don't consider their current benefits—generous retirement plans and health insurance policies included. Instead, they focus on the carrot in front of them, whatever it may be: securing better working conditions, landing an impressive title, making more money, improving their commute. Unfortunately, those things don't necessarily pay off overall.

Before you make a big move, make sure to evaluate what you'd be giving up if you changed roles. Even if the position you're up for comes with a larger paycheck, you may be losing out on a significant amount of cash on the back end. For example, if you're a teacher or a government employee, then you could be sacrificing a big pension by transitioning to a different profession. Your new company may offer another kind of retirement plan, such as a 401(k), but by giving up that pension—and particularly a defined benefit plan—you'll probably be losing out on a lot of money, since pensions typically pay significantly more over the life of your investment. Maybe you don't have a pension plan, but your employer offers a hefty retirement match, netting you thousands of dollars each year in free money. If your future job doesn't provide the same opportunity, then you might end up making less than you would over time even if you bring home a bigger paycheck.

If some portion of your retirement benefits is on the table when you're considering a move, really think it through. Would you be fully vested if you waited just a few more years? If so, it might be worth sticking it out, since you'll have a lot more security with those extra funds. Andrea made this mistake. She was leaving her teaching job at a public school to join an education technology startup. The company boasted a number of perks—new offices in bustling part of the city, free gourmet lunch, and other features that made it seem far more appealing than heating up frozen meals every day in the crumbling teachers' lounge at her suburban school. More important, they had offered her $20,000 more than she had been making, and she was excited to have the additional cash. However, like most for-profit organizations, the company wouldn't be offering a pension—she'd have a 401(k), which she would have to fund entirely on her own, and it would have been only three more years until she was vested in her previous plan. Ultimately, she'd lose out on about $15,000 per year in retirement. Over the course of thirty years, she'd give up nearly half a million dollars to make $20,000 more today.

It's also important to think about the stability of the company you're moving to. Is it big or small? How many years has it been in operation? If it goes under shortly after you sign on, and you find yourself scrambling to find a new job, would you still be glad that you left your old one?

I certainly don't want to dissuade you from following your

passion, but if it's money that's driving your decision, make sure to consider every aspect of your move and whether it will really benefit you in the long run. You don't want to be in a situation where you're taking one step forward only to take two steps back when retirement rolls around, or if your new company dissolves entirely.

WATCH OUT WHEN YOU MOVE RETIREMENT FUNDS

If you do decide to take a new job, it's up to you to move your retirement money, too. But be aware of any differences between your previous plan and your new one before you transfer the funds. For example, a client of mine recently took a new job and wanted to roll the savings in his old account into his current employer's plan. The catch? He had a Roth 401(k), in which contributions are made on a post-tax basis, and his new employer offered a traditional 401(k), where taxes would be levied once funds were withdrawn. If he had made the transfer without talking to me first, he would have ended up paying taxes twice—once before the money went into his original Roth account and again when he pulled it out of his traditional IRA plan at retirement.

You also want to look at other aspects of a new plan, including how old you have to be before you can begin taking distributions. For example, if you have a 457(b) plan—a government retirement plan—then you can withdraw your money at any time without incurring a penalty. Meanwhile, 403(b) plans, which are often offered at nonprofits, allow you to take deductions beginning at age fifty-five. If you move funds from either of those accounts to a traditional IRA or 401(k), then you'll have to wait until you hit age 59.5 to take earnings out without a penalty. This is just one thing to keep in mind when you're coordinating such a change.

SET UP YOUR OWN ACCOUNT

In a climate where moving from one employer to another is common, it's smart to have your own retirement account, as well—separate from what your company offers. If you haven't done it yet, set up your own fund outside of your job in addition to whatever you're being offered at work. That way, future transitions can be made more smoothly, since you can always save in your own plan. Employers are also doing less and less for their employees these days, so you may find that your new role doesn't even offer a retirement savings plan, making it all the more crucial to have one for yourself.

With any job change, there are other elements to consider. It's like leaving one relationship and jumping into the next—it's up to you to ensure you're making the best choice you can. Sometimes, the grass isn't as green as it looked from the other side. If you're making 10 percent more money per year, but you end up spending it on higher taxes and the gas and car maintenance involved in a longer commute, making the switch didn't really do any good, did it?

Kevin's experience serves as the perfect example. He was all too happy to leave his government job for a new corporate gig that paid about $10,000 more per year. He figured the cushy office in addition to the salary bump would be worth it. But with a pricier health-care plan, a longer commute, and a few other factors, Kevin quickly found that he was spending virtually all of the increase that came with the position. The new company also didn't offer an employee match toward retirement, so he wasn't any better off in the long run.

To avoid a situation like Kevin's, make sure that when you leave to go to a better-paying job you're not unknowingly hindering yourself. There are a few things you can do to ensure a smooth and successful transition:

- If your company offers a retirement plan, enroll as soon as possible to continue saving for tomorrow.

- Making more money? Contribute at least part of that increase toward your future by putting a greater amount into your retirement fund each month. If your employer provides a match, do everything you can to take full advantage of it—maxing out their offering with your own contributions.

- Banking on additional benefits like a shorter commute to make life better in a new role? Get even more out of lifestyle enhancements by contributing anything you save on gas and car repairs toward an emergency or retirement fund.

- Need help deciphering all of the offerings that come with a new opportunity? Find someone who can help you navigate your options to avoid losing money unnecessarily. Members of your company's benefits department, financial advisors, and friends and family members who are savvy in this area can all be a big help.

WEIGH THE PROS AND CONS OF GOING BACK TO SCHOOL

Are you considering a new career that requires further education? Determine whether it's worth it to start from scratch. Even though education can be an excellent investment in yourself, it doesn't always have the same effect on your income. Many people don't anticipate the cost and time commitment of going back to school, especially if they've been out of the classroom for a while. But if you're heading into something like teaching, where your new degree will allow you access to a career with stability and significant benefits you'd have missed out on otherwise, then you may have to pay a bit more up front, but you'll end profiting in the end.

To find out if going back to school is right for you, do your research. Find out how much the program you're interested in costs at different institutions. And for some insight on the true value of the program, check out the earning potential for people who pursue a similar degree or career path. You should also look into the time commitment associated with each program you're considering. Are there part-time options that would allow you to keep working, or is full-time the only way to go? Recent alumni, current students, and the school's admissions officers can also give you an idea of how many hours you'll spend on your studies. With a strong sense of what an education could provide, you're ready to make an informed decision about whether more schooling is right for you.

WHAT TO THINK ABOUT WHEN YOU'RE THINKING OF STARTING A BUSINESS

Thinking of striking out on your own and opening a business? I don't blame you. Setting your own hours, working for yourself, doing something you care about—it all sounds pretty appealing. Unfortunately, for most people, becoming their own boss is usually not a good idea. The difficult truth is that most businesses fail—20 percent in the first year, 30 percent in their second year, 50 percent by year five, and a whopping 70 percent within ten years.[43] People usually overextend themselves in the process, taking out small-business loans

---

43 Georgia McIntyre, "What Is the Small Business Failure Rate?" *Fundera*, November 26, 2018, www.fundera.com/blog/what-percentage-of-small-businesses-fail.

and engaging in other practices that land them in massive debt that lasts long after their doors are shut.

Of course, starting a business isn't always a bad decision. After all, I made it myself. I had been working as an elementary school PE teacher for three years at the time, and after working with a friend who was an advisor to get my own finances in order, I thought it might be the right path for me, too. But I did a lot of homework and took my circumstances into account before I made the jump.

I knew I wouldn't be vested in my pension plan until I hit year ten of teaching. Since I was only twenty-four years old and single at the time, without any kids, it didn't seem worth it to wait another seven years before setting out on my own. I also owned my home— something few young people can say today—and I was renting out the extra bedrooms to friends, covering most of mortgage and keeping my overhead low. I had the financial flexibility to spend a couple of years making very little money and the availability to work crazy hours to get my business up and running. I had also made a plan to cover on my own all of the benefits that my previous job offered. I was ready to pay for my own health insurance and manage my retirement, and I had built up an emergency fund to deal with the inconsistent income inherent in early business ownership. If I had had a spouse and children at the time, then it would have been much more of a challenge to make it all work.

It's essential to consider your situation and the business you're planning to start. Are there particular ebbs and flows to be aware of? Would you be slammed at Christmas but hear crickets all summer, and could you manage both the chaos and quiet successfully? Would your potential business be seasonal, requiring you to find a part-time gig six months out of the year? And would a recession leave you struggling to find any work at all? As a hairstylist, you may have regular clients no matter what the market's doing, but if you're running something recreational—like a skydiving company—then business may drop off if people aren't doing as well as they used to. All of these elements are important in determining whether entrepreneurship is right for you.

Evan learned this directly. Evan had always dreamed about starting his own restaurant—a fine-dining establishment—in his small hometown. Cooking was his passion, and as the years ticked by, he grappled with the growing feeling that he was just wasting time. He was good at his job, it paid well and offered him plenty of stability, but he just wasn't happy. When an old pizza shop closed just down the street from where he grew up—one that had a huge dining room and a wood-fired oven, he decided it was time to take a risk and follow his dream.

Evan cashed out his 401(k), paying taxes and a 10 percent penalty on the money, and used it to fund his venture. Then he rented the space and got to work outfitting it with high-end appliances and furnishings. When he first opened, he was the talk of the town. Everything seemed promising. He was featured in the local newspapers, and he had customers filling seats every night of the week. But even with a full house, he was just treading water. He knew restaurants had high overheads, but he hadn't anticipated just how high they could be. He was barely breaking even. When business began to slow months later, his business was in the red.

It turns out his town didn't really need a high-end restaurant; all his neighbors really wanted were coffee shops and breakfast spots. Once the buzz died down, the only people who came were celebrating special events—particularly because his prices were pretty high. And they had to be, because the cost of operating was astronomical. Evan spent the next few years trying to make his dream work, depleting all of his savings in the process. In the end, he had to close his doors. Since he didn't own the space, there was nothing left of the business and nothing left of his savings. He'd have to start over—likely in a position very similar to the one he'd left.

You've probably heard stories that have turned out just the opposite: about people who ventured out on their own with a thousand bucks, an idea, and zero experience and created a billion-dollar business. Of course, those cases are out there, but they're the exceptions to the rule. I'm not saying that you shouldn't pursue what makes your heart beat faster, but if you do, ensure that your finances are a key part of your vision.

You also need to think about the long game, even if your business *is* successful. What happens if you get tired of running things, or you want to retire? If what you've built is entirely based on your own skill set, there may not be anything to sell when you're ready to move on. If you're a real estate agent and you've built a booming business over the course of your career, then it's still just you at the end of the day, and if you're done working there's nothing to buy. It may be a different story if you've invested in a car dealership or salon. It those cases, you probably have inventory, equipment, customers—all elements that have value to a potential buyer.

START SMALL

If you do decide that launching your own enterprise is the only way to go, my number-one recommendation is to keep your overhead low. When you're on your own, a penny saved really is a penny earned. The best way to do this is to start small. Starting small means that you don't have to worry as much about generating revenue to pay the bills. Begin with just yourself, if possible, and handle all of the administrative duties on your own until you're bringing in enough money to afford real help. If you can use a space in your home for your fledgling business rather than renting one, then do that, too.

An even better proposition? Keeping your current job while starting something new. By holding on to a regular role, you don't lose it all if things don't go according to plan. If it's not feasible to do both at the same time, then make sure you have enough financial cushion to get you through storms and slow months, since your income is bound to fluctuate. I'd recommend having enough to take care of your expenses for at least a year.

BE YOUR OWN BENEFITS ADMINISTRATOR

If you're starting your own business, keep in mind that you'll have to make up for any benefits an employer was providing. And when you're on your own, without the backing of a big organization, those benefits tend to cost more. Perhaps your health insurance was $300 per month, since your previous company chipped in on your behalf. Purchasing it on your own might cost $700. That's an extra $4,800 annually that you must account for. If you were receiving a $2,000 or $3,000 retirement match per year, you should be working to make up the difference yourself, so that your savings don't take a big hit. Ask yourself whether you have the time, energy, and resources to be your own benefits administrator, and be honest about the answer. When you're working for yourself, it's not just your livelihood; it's your whole life.

DON'T SKIP OUT ON SAVING FOR RETIREMENT

When you're the boss, it's up to you to put money away for retirement—no one is going to do it for you. I work with plenty of couples where one spouse works for himself or herself—doctors, lawyers, music teachers, nail technicians. They run successful ventures, but they don't save anything for the future. Everything is tied up in the business itself. If they were to walk away today, they'd have nothing. You don't have to face a similar fate. In addition to the retirement plans we discussed in Chapter 4, there are other options available to you as a business owner or independent contractor:

- *Solo 401(k)s*: Solo 401(k)s are pretty much what they sound like: personal 401(k) plans. They're available to business owners who don't have any employees, as well as to the owner's spouse.[44] The plan operates just like a regular 401(k) plan. However, since you're technically the plan administrator, too, you can match your own contributions, meaning you can add even more than a 401(k) plan would allow.[45]

- *SEP IRAs*: SEP IRAs, or Simplified Employee Pensions, allow you to contribute to your own retirement, as well as to the retirement of any employees you may have on board. The plan operates similarly to a traditional IRA, and the same set of rules applies.[46] Your money is taxed upon distribution, and withdrawals can begin without penalty at age 59.5. With these plans, you can also contribute up to 20 percent of your income before taxes.[47] SEPs are available to businesses of all sizes, and they don't have the high operational costs that conventional retirement plans do—a

---

44   "One-Participant 401(k) Plans," *Internal Revenue Service*, www.irs.gov/ retirement-plans/one-participant-401k-plans.

45   Melissa Phipps, "Self-Employed Retirement Plans," *The Balance*, February 15, 2017, www.thebalance.com/self-employed-retirement-plans-2894523.

46   "SEP Plan FAQs," *IRS*. www.irs.gov/retirement-plans/ retirement-plans-faqs-regarding-seps

47   Phipps, "Self-Employed Retirement Plans."

major benefit for small businesses with limited resources. It's important to note that if you do have employees, only you—the employer—can make contributions. While the contribution rate must be the same for everyone in your organization, the amount you put in can fluctuate, meaning that during years when you don't bring as much in, you can pay less toward the plan.[48]

- *Simple IRAs*: Simple IRAs, or Savings Incentive Match Plans for Employees, are available to businesses with one hundred or fewer employees. These plans also follow the same rules that come with a traditional IRA. However, with simple IRAs, employees can make their own contributions, and employers are required to provide a match—up to 3 percent of salaries for employees who contribute to the plan and 2 percent for employees who don't contribute.[49]

Before you choose a plan, make sure to familiarize yourself with all of the relevant costs to maintain it, and think about the characteristics that may make one type of plan more or less suited to your needs than another.

KEEP YOUR FAMILY—AND FUTURE—IN MIND

Regardless of the career change you're making—switching roles, going back to school, or starting a company—your spouse and family must be on board, too, since any changes you make will inevitably affect them. I'm all for entrepreneurship, but it's up to you to make

---

48 "Choosing a Retirement Plan: SEP," *IRS*, www.irs.gov/retirement-plans/ choosing-a-retirement-plan-sep.

49 "Choosing a Retirement Plan: SIMPLE IRA Plan," *IRS*, www.irs.gov/ retirement-plans/choosing-a-retirement-plan-simple-ira-plan.

sure that your venture is as sustainable as it can be, especially if others are depending you. Your ultimate goal at this point in life is still to set yourself up for those golden years. That means doing all you can to make your future plans possible, whatever they are.

MANAGING OTHER MIDLIFE CHANGES

There is a slew of other changes that people find themselves managing as they reach those middle years, many of which can't be predicted. I've seen numerous clients wind up getting divorced, assuming responsibility for a grandchild, or working to catch up after making a midlife-crisis-fueled purchase like a luxury vehicle. While you can't necessarily plan for these things, you can consider the potential costs associated with them and use that as inspiration to save more for the just-in-case scenarios that may come your way. Let's run through some of the midlife changes people commonly experience and the expenses associated with each.

DIVORCE

We've all heard that in the US, more than half of all marriages end in divorce. Though few people imagine their marriages ending, odds are even that they will. And, unfortunately, along with the heartache that accompanies the end of a marriage is the high cost of divorce itself—averaging about $15,500 in America—as well as any court-ordered payments, such as alimony, which can go on for years.[50] If children are involved, expect to pay even more, since one party will probably end up saddled with child support. I have clients paying in

---

50   Samuel Stebbins, "How Much Does It Cost to Get a Divorce? 10 States with the Highest Price Tags." *USA Today,* November 26, 2018, www.usatoday.com/story/money/2018/11/26/how-much-does-cost-get-divorce-most-expensive-states/38446243.

excess of $1,500 per month in child support alone. And that money comes out after taxes—not before. You can't exactly plan for divorce, but you can educate yourself on the financial burden associated with it, and let that knowledge drive your behavior. That might involve padding your emergency fund a bit more or investing in a marriage counselor if things get tough between you and your spouse.

SUPPORTING GRANDCHILDREN

Many people end up helping support their grandchildren, either by pitching in financially or by providing care themselves. If caring for extended family seems like it might be in the cards for you, then understand what it would take to absorb the added cost. Outsourcing childcare can be a five-figure expense per year. And if you're the one who will be watching your grandkids, then you'll probably need to work fewer hours to be there for them—meaning less income for you. Do these scenarios sound less than ideal? Make sure to educate your children about finances so that there's a smaller chance you'll have to support their children later on.

BIG MIDLIFE PURCHASES

As you near retirement, you may be interested in making a big purchase for yourself. Perhaps your kids have left the nest, or you've been working hard for a very long time, and you feel you deserve to do something just for you. By all means go for it, as long as making that choice won't interfere with your future. Sports cars, boats, exotic vacations—it's great to treat yourself if you can afford it. But you don't want to end up in a situation where you have to drain your savings account or borrow on your retirement fund to make an extravagant purchase, especially with just a handful of working years left before you plan to retire. I've seen people end up staying in their jobs for many more years than they wanted to because they had to pay off an ill-advised buy.

GET THE MOST OUT OF MIDLIFE, NO MATTER WHAT YOU DO

The moral of the story is to be smart about any decision you make. Be aware of the true expenses associated with your choices, and save as much as you can along the way to cushion yourself in case something you didn't predict happens. Here's a quick rundown of things to keep in mind when you're changing careers or altering your circumstances in the middle of your life:

- *Don't make a move without thinking it through.* This applies to most any situation that might arise during those middle years, but especially to your career. It's easy to fall into the trap of believing that things will be better somewhere else, but be aware of what you'd be giving up—and getting in return—before making a particular decision.

- *Pay attention if you're moving retirement funds.* If you're switching jobs and you have an employer-sponsored retirement fund, then you'll have to move that money, too. But be careful when you do: you need to know the difference between current and previous plans to avoid paying unnecessary fees, taxes, and penalties.

- *Consider the pros and cons when it comes to going back to school.* A new career that requires more education could provide you with significant value and security—or it could simply sap your time and funds and offer little in return.

Make sure you understand what you'll be sacrificing in terms of both time and money, and determine the costs and benefits before you dive into a new program.

- *Don't let a new business turn into a money pit.* For most people, opening up a business is not the way to go. The vast majority of them fail within ten years. But if you can't help but follow your passion, then make sure you're prepared. Build up your savings, keep your overhead low, and make sure to account for any benefits previously covered by your employer, such as health insurance, life insurance, and retirement.

- *Keep saving to handle anything unexpected.* Many changes arise during midlife, and you can't always prepare for them. What you can do is ready yourself for any additional costs by continuing to save for a rainy day. For more tips on how to plan for the unexpected, check out Chapter 6.

You've put so much work into that little tree already, and it's not quite harvest time yet. These are still your earning years. It's okay to make some changes during this time, but do what you can to ensure that your choices today don't have too much of an impact on your ability to enjoy things later on. In the next chapter, we'll tackle what happens when it's finally quitting time, including how to ensure that all your hard work will sustain you for the rest of your life.

CHAPTER 8

MANAGING YOUR RETIREMENT

I f you've done it right, you've been tending to your finances and your future, growing yourself a tree that will provide fruit for the rest of your life. It's time to slow down, sit back, and reap the benefits of your hard work. Congratulations!

But before you get too comfortable, remember that your savings must last as long as you do. With a US average life expectancy of nearly eighty years, you could be in retirement for two or more decades. If your cash dries up too fast, then you're in real trouble.[51] That potential is even scarier when you consider that one in four sixty-five-year-olds will live to be at least aged ninety, and one in ten

51 K. Kochanek, S. Murphy, J. Xu, and E. Arias. "Mortality in the United States," National Center for Health Statistics, 2016. www.cdc.gov/nchs/data/databriefs/db293.pdf

will reach age ninety-five.[52] You don't want to be in a situation where you have to head back to work, seek support from family members, or rely on government programs just to get by. Fortunately, there are steps you can take to make your money last; it just requires a little bit of foresight and some more... work.

BE CAREFUL ABOUT SPENDING

With the knowledge that your money is going to have to last a while, it's crucial to be careful with your spending. In theory, this is relatively easy—many people find that their expenses are actually lower in retirement than before. If your home and car are paid off and your kids are out of the house, then you won't have nearly as many bills to worry about as you did in your younger days. While you may have less income in retirement, as long as you have fewer expenses, it's all good. To determine whether this is the case for you, look at your net cash flow. Maybe you're bringing in $800 less per month than when you were working, but without any additional mouths to feed and a car that's all yours, you're saving about $1,200 in expenses. That means you actually have $400 a month more to work with than you had before. At this point, it's not so much about income as it is about overhead. To make sure that you're in a position to boost or maintain your bottom line, put energy into downsizing in retirement. If you do so, then you'll have nothing to worry about.

Unfortunately, this wasn't the case for my client Bea. Bea's job was stressful and, as a result, she had decided to retire a little bit early. Even though it would be tight, she and I both thought she'd be

---

52   Michelle Singletary, "Your Long Life Could Be the Death of Your Retirement Savings," *Washington Post,* April 9, 2018. www.washingtonpost.com/news/get-there/wp/2018/04/09/your-long-life-could-be-the-death-of-your-retirement-savings/?utm_term=.e59178a3298a

covered, because she planned to spend less money in retirement. In terms of paying off her big bills—car payment, mortgage, debt—she was all set. In addition, I had worked with her to put her money in long-term investments, where it was supposed to stay and grow, giving her more funds over time.

But what Bea didn't account for was all of the extra hours she would have. Work had kept her busy, and with nothing to do from morning till night, she was out shopping, eating with friends, and traveling to see her grandchildren. As a result, she was spending much more money than when she was working.

Bea was depleting her retirement savings at a rapid rate, *and* burning through her emergency fund. Whenever she called me to take out cash, she hid the circumstances of her spending, claiming she needed the money for medical expenses and other necessities. Each time, she promised it would be the last, but unfortunately it never was. Because the market was down while she was making these withdrawals, she was losing even more. In less than three years, she had used almost all of her savings. All that was left was a small pension, which didn't even cover her basic expenses. Her only option? To find a job. Now she works part-time at a big box retailer, and she'll never be able to put back what she took out. Plus, because she's relatively healthy, there's a good chance she'll live a long time. At some point, she'll have to stop working and depend on her children to make ends meet.

Like Bea, many people's retirement plans aren't equipped to handle unnecessary purchases. But Edwin didn't consider this reality when he pulled out a significant portion of his savings to buy a new car—something that was not at all part of our plan. We had discussed at length that to make it through, he'd need to continue driving his current vehicle and live below his means. However, he felt he'd worked so hard and for so long that he deserved an upgrade. He didn't quite understand how high the price tag would be when it came to his future.

Edwin was also unaware of just how much inflation would impact his savings. Things simply cost more over time. At that particular point, gas prices and health insurance costs were going up, while home values were dropping. The worth of his assets was decreasing, while his expenses were continuing to grow. Moreover, his new car was quite the gas guzzler. With a big dent in the plan we'd built together, Edwin also chose to return to work, and he was grateful—and lucky—that his company agreed to have him back. Today, he's still there, with no clock-out date in sight.

When people finally have access to their retirement money—often hundreds of thousands of dollars—it can be hard for them to exercise self-control and only take what they need, especially if they previously lived month to month. Looking at numbers like that, it's easy to convince yourself that the money will never run out, but it goes much more quickly than you think. While it's tempting to spend on a new car, vacations, or any number of shiny objects that you may not have been able to access before, it's important to remember that the money you have must last, and that the real big-ticket item you have to prepare for is rising health care costs.

WATCH OUT FOR RISING HEALTH CARE COSTS

Consider this powerful stat: a sixty-five-year-old couple will have an average of $10,700 in health-related expenses per year. By the time they reach age eighty-five, that couple can expect to pay almost three-

and-a-half times as much in health care costs—about \$37,500![53] If those numbers don't convey the impact health care can have on your pocketbook as you age, then I don't know what will. Clients come to me all the time for help managing the added expense of procedures that aren't covered by insurance. This is just another factor to consider when you're weighing the pros and cons of an expensive purchase in retirement. What if you find yourself footing the bill for recurring medical treatments for yourself or your spouse, or even long-term care? If you wouldn't be able to handle the cost of both a boat and health-related expenses, then think twice before calling yourself "captain."

> **IF YOU WOULDN'T BE ABLE TO HANDLE THE COST OF BOTH A BOAT AND HEALTH-RELATED EXPENSES, THEN THINK TWICE BEFORE CALLING YOURSELF "CAPTAIN."**

If you don't have an emergency fund, then now is the time to get one. With health care expenses that are almost guaranteed to increase and the other inevitable incidents that require extra spending, such as home and car repairs, it's extremely helpful to have a separate fund that you can pull from. If you're taking money from the same place when something big comes up, you'll end up poking a hole in your bucket, and that savings will drain out faster than you may be able to afford. Having an emergency fund puts less pressure on your retirement fund, keeping you in a better position over time.

---

53   "Talk, Plan, Act: Guiding Your Clients to a Financially Secure Retirement," *OppenheimerFunds*, 2018. https://www.oppenheimerfunds.com/advisors/da/ Talk_Plan_Act_Retirement_Chart_Book_-_CE.pdf

STICK TO THE PLAN FOR SMOOTH SAILING

While the scenarios above are somewhat depressing to think about, it's certainly not all gloom and doom. If you stick to the plan and continue to spend and save responsibly, then retirement can be smooth sailing. With the money you've saved—and lower expenses—you can live comfortably on your own terms. That's the case for Rebecca, a retired nurse in her seventies. Rebecca contributed about $300,000 to her retirement account over the course of her career, which has grown to almost $500,000. She's taken out $200,000 to live on, but the rest remains in her account. She probably won't outlive that money, putting her in a very good situation.

I keep an eye on Rebecca's account balance. Since she's in such a stable position with more money than she'll be able to use, I've actually encouraged her to take a bit more out, so that she can have fun when she's healthy. Because her spouse and kids are self-sufficient, even if she spends most of what's left in the next ten to fifteen years, it won't be an issue. That's the goal: to have as much as you need per month, with a bit left over to play with or leave to your loved ones, depending on your goals.

When you're comfortable, you can choose how you spend your time—vacationing, seeing family and friends, relaxing, playing golf, or even finding a low-stress job you enjoy. There are plenty of people who go back to work part-time, just to have something to do. With some extra income, they have a little more money to play with in case they want to spend more on little luxuries.

Most of my clients end up in situations like Rebecca's. They retire, their bills are in line, and they're able to make their monthly obligations. They put anything they don't spend back in the bank or use it for travel, leisure, and the like. These are the kinds of situations

I shoot for. I tell people all the time, "I'm not going to try to make you rich, but you won't have to worry about the poor house." In the end, however, no matter how solid a plan you have, you're the only one who can determine your future.

If you need a reminder about how important it is to stick to it, pick out a single item that you use in your everyday life—a stamp, a carton of milk, a loaf of bread—and see how the price has changed over ten, twenty, or fifty years. You'll see inflation at work. Prices are going to continue to go up, and to stay afloat, you need to make sure the money you've saved is continuing to work for you.[54]

COST CONSIDERATIONS OF A LONGER LIFESPAN

Cost Projection for Healthcare[1]
Includes Medicare Parts B, D Supplemental, and all out-of-pocket costs, including deductibles and co-pays)

Percentage of Seniors Living in a Nursing Home[2]

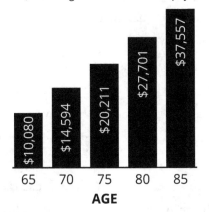

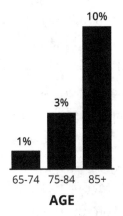

AGE

AGE

INFLATION

 Movie Tickets[3]
$4.22 vs $8.73

Coffee[4]
$2.94 vs $4.28

 Gallon of Milk[4]
$2.78 vs $3.19

1. Source: Healthview Insigts: 2016 Retirement Health Care Costs Data Report.
2. Source: Administration on Aging "A Profile of Older Americans" 2014.
3. Source: National Association of Theatre Owners, 2016.
4. Source: Bureau of Labor Statistics, 2017.

54   "Talk, Plan, Act: Guiding Your Clients to a Financially Secure Retirement," *Oppen-heimerFunds*, 2018.

If you do hit a snag along the way in the form of an ill-advised purchase or a costly health issue, it's still possible to get back on track, but it requires a conscious effort. Think of it this way: if a pothole in the road sends your car out of alignment, then you have two options. You can either fix it for a nominal amount, or just keep driving. If you go with the latter choice, then that car is eventually going to give out. The same goes for your retirement. I work with people all the time who are overwhelmed by the numbers and withdraw too much. The difference between those who are able to turn it around and those who end up as Walmart greeters or restaurant workers in their seventies and eighties is whether they make a course correction.

CELEBRATE YOUR WINS

On occasion, things work out even better than planned, and it's worth celebrating those moments. I had the privilege of calling Howard to tell him that he was in great financial shape. Howard had been prudent during his career, saving money whenever he could. He was putting some of his earnings in the bank, but he also had investments, and those had grown significantly over time. Why did his investments do so well? He left them alone, even when the market went down. Many investors don't do this. Fear and emotions cause them to pull out their money when the going gets tough. But the reality is that those people are almost guaranteed to do much worse than the market itself. The typical investor averages about a 2.6 percent rate of return on their money over the course of thirty years. But US stocks average 10.2 percent, demonstrating that leaving funds where they are is the safest—and smartest—bet you can make.[55] To get an idea

---

55   "Compelling Wealth Management Conversations," *Oppenheimer-Funds*, 2018, www.oppenheimerfunds.com/advisors/article/conversations-compelling-wealth-management.

of how the average investor performs compared to the market as a whole, check out the information below.

Howard's commitment to leaving his money in its place meant that when the market rebounded, his funds were ready and able to grow. Because his money has done so well, he's more than set to weather the challenges of inflation. He won't even have to touch his retirement fund until he reaches 70.5, the age when he is required to begin taking withdrawals. There are plenty of stories like Howard's. Here are just two:

- I work with Susan and James, who were both in the military. When they were done with their service, they both got jobs in other fields and continued to save toward retirement in 401(k)s. Today, they get a pension and health care through the military, and everything else is icing on the cake.

- Ralph worked in corporate America, and when he retired, he downsized to a smaller home, primarily because he was divorced and his kids were grown. As a result, he has fewer bills, which aren't even putting a dent in the millions of dollars he has saved. He takes out just 4 percent of his savings per year on top of the social security he receives, bringing in nearly $100,000 annually. He uses that money to do what he loves: fishing, hunting, and camping.

STRATEGIES TO STAY ALIGNED

Great circumstances like these—and those of clients who are simply able to live comfortably—come down to two things: saving well for retirement, and maintaining those efforts once you stop working.

Here are some strategies you can use to keep your retirement on track:

- *Hold off on taking distributions if you can.* If you can avoid taking a distribution for a while, do it. Waiting a bit longer will allow your money to grow, giving it the kind of longevity you may need down the line.

- *When you do start withdrawing, take out small amounts.* Taking smaller distributions means your money can last longer. I suggest starting in the 4 percent range. As your overhead goes down and you're paying things off—a home, a car, or any existing debt—see if you can reduce that distribution amount even further.

- *Keep an eye on your balance.* As you're taking distributions, watch your balance. Based on how the account performs, consider making some adjustments—whether that's taking out a little more each month if you're doing very well, cutting back a bit if you're spending too fast, or even pausing to let your money grow.

- *Use a second account for emergencies.* If you haven't set up an emergency account yet, now's the time. That way, if something comes up, you won't have to siphon extra funds from your retirement account, helping those dollars last.

- *Plan on retirement costing more than you thought.* Remember the impact of inflation? Prices will continue to rise after you've stopped working, and you need to account for that in retirement. With today's life spans, it's possible that a two-, three-, or four-decade retirement may be a reality for you. If you prepare for life to cost a little more than it does currently by spending less, then you'll be in a better position when your expenses rise due to inflation.

- *Have an ownership stake in something that will beat rising rates.* Inflation is inevitable. You need to have money invested in something that will grow along with rising costs. If you have all your cash in the bank, getting a 1 percent return, then you're not going to be able to keep up with a rate that's rising at 2 or 3 percent.

- *Work with an advisor.* This stuff can be complicated. It's hard to know exactly how to save or invest your money to ensure you have everything you need after quitting time. An advisor can make a big difference, giving you a roadmap to help you arrive at your final destination. After that, it's up to you, but it can be invaluable to have an expert point you in the right direction to begin with.

You've already done the work. That tree is strong and sturdy. You just have to make sure it stays that way. If you end up harvesting more fruit than you meant to, then work to get back on track, taking a little less the next time around. And if you need help, don't be afraid to reach out. These days, life is long, but you have the tools you need to create enough shade and sustenance for years to come.

CHAPTER 9

SOIL AND SEEDS: THINKING ABOUT END-OF-LIFE FINANCES

A s we near the end of our time together, it's time to discuss a challenging topic: end-of-life plans. While it can be hard to think about leaving friends and family behind, it's important to prepare for the future—even one without you in it—so that you don't make things more difficult for the ones you love most. Doing it the right way means ensuring that you're able to manage the cost of any care you might need and final expenses, as well as taking some time to determine the legacy you want to leave behind.

There are plenty of ways not only to live the life you want, but also to create something that lasts long after you're gone—whether it's in the form of strong memories and quality time or financial support. But first, you have to determine your goals. Do you want to spend any extra money on experiences? Would you rather be more conservative and have funds left over for your children, grandchildren, and/or a charity that you're passionate about? Maybe you're aiming for a mix of both. No matter what you want to accomplish, you never know what tomorrow might hold. The more you can do now to ready yourself for the end, the better off you'll be.

Let's discuss some potential end-of-life scenarios and the arrangements you can make to achieve them, starting with something that's unpleasant but often necessary: long-term care and final expenses.

LONG-TERM CARE AND FINAL EXPENSES

Many of us reach a point where we can't care for ourselves on our own. Who will oversee your affairs—physical and financial—if you don't have the capacity to handle them yourself someday? Everyday tasks such as bathing, dressing, and managing personal finances fall under the umbrella of long-term care, a service you may very well need. This is especially true if you don't have a spouse or kids to rely on for help, or if you don't want to be a burden to them down the road.

Outsourcing long-term care is quite expensive, with an average cost of $68 per day for time spent in an adult day health care center, and $225 per day—or $6,844 per month—for a shared room in a nursing home.[56] Worse, you can't count on insurance to cover those costs. Most plans, including Medicare, don't cover most long-term care expenses. As such, those who don't think about and plan for these services in advance often create a tough situation for their families,

---

56 "Costs of Care," *US Department of Health and Human Services Administration on Aging*, https://longtermcare.acl.gov/costs-how-to-pay/costs-of-care.html.

who end up either shouldering the high cost of long-term care—to their own financial detriment—or providing the support themselves.

There are certain factors that increase the likelihood that you'll need long-term care. Those who are older, women (who live an average of five years longer than men), people with disabilities and/ or chronic conditions such as diabetes and high blood pressure, and those who live alone are more likely to need long-term care.[57] If you fall into one of those categories, then you should definitely think about how to account for the additional expense. If your retirement fund can't handle such steep prices, you can purchase long-term care insurance, which is built to provide for the support traditional health care plans don't cover. Pricing depends on your age and the maximum cost and duration of care that the plan will absorb.[58]

Alina understands the importance of planning firsthand. Her mother, Vickie, failed to prepare for the future. Today, Alina is working to take care of Vickie on her own. Vickie lived in a different part of town, and when she first got sick, Alina was commuting to her home every day to take care of her. When Vicki could still be alone for a portion of the day, it was manageable, but as her illness progressed, she began to need around-the-clock support. While Alina could afford to pay for a home health aid part time, she couldn't handle the cost of having someone there twenty-four hours a day. As a result, she's had to take an early retirement and move in with her mother to provide some assistance herself. While Alina is fortunate to have a good pension plan—and Vicki is lucky to have such a dedicated daughter—more prep on Vicki's part, such as the purchase of a long-term care plan, could have helped them avoid this situation.

---

57   Ibid.

58   "What Is Long-term Care Insurance?" *US Department of Health and Human Services Administration on Aging*, https://longtermcare.acl.gov/costs-how-to-pay/what-is-long-term-care-insurance/index.html.

Another costly consideration: final expenses. In the US, the median cost of a funeral and burial is $7,360, but experts recommend setting aside $10,000 to account for any additional expenses that aren't part of a basic arrangement. Families can use money from life insurance plans to pay for it, but if you don't have a life insurance policy (or you purchased term insurance that has already ended), and you don't think you'll have enough money set aside, then you may want to consider final expense insurance. The benefit usually tops out around $20,000 and is meant to be used for a funeral and other relevant charges, such as medical bills.[59] You also name a beneficiary on policies such as these, allowing your loved one, or even a funeral home in some cases, to access any funds right away so they don't have to front the money themselves.

TO SAVE OR TO SPEND

Once you've ensured that you have a plan for health care and final expenses, you have two choices. You can either spend the money you have while you're alive, or you can think about how much you'd like to leave behind, and to whom (or what). While it may seem selfish to choose the first option, if you don't have any family, or if your children and spouse are doing very well on their own, then it may make sense to use your cash while you still can.

If your goal is to support a child, family member, friend, or organization after you're gone, then think realistically about the assets you'll have at the end of your life and how you want to divide them up. Everyone's situation is different: maybe splitting your money evenly between your children makes sense. Perhaps one of your

---

59   Amelia Josephson, " What Is Final Expense Insurance?" *smartasset*, May 21, 2018, https://smartasset.com/life-insurance/final-expense-insurance.

kids struggles with addiction, and leaving him a large inheritance would be dangerous to his health. While you leave your other kids cash, passing your home on to him may be a better idea. You might decide to contribute equally to your grandchildren's education, or determine that one child in particular could really benefit from your contribution, while the others will have more than enough support from their parents.

Once you've identified your goals, you can determine your lifestyle in retirement. If you're planning to spend your money while you're alive, all you have to do is worry about covering your own expenses. But if you want to have something left over, you must take that into account, too. That may mean taking fewer vacations, moving to a smaller place, or making other decisions that further reduce your expenditures.

PROVIDING FUNDS FOR LOVED ONES

Curtis fell into the latter camp: he wanted to leave something behind for his two children. After weighing his circumstances, he decided that the best way to make an impact was to purchase a single-premium life insurance plan. With this type of plan, he could purchase a set amount of permanent life insurance and guarantee that when he died, his children would receive more money than what he had set aside to leave them.

With a single-premium life insurance plan, the money is invested all at once. As a result, it grows quickly. Death benefits are determined based on the buyer's age and health—essentially the amount of time the money has to grow.[60] Because Curtis was healthy and in his sixties, he was able to pay $50,000 for a $100,000 plan, doubling

---

60 George D. Lambert, "A Look at Single-Premium Life Insurance," *Investopedia*, May 31, 2018, www.investopedia.com/articles/pf/05/singlepremlife.asp.

his children's inheritance upon his death. The other benefit of any kind of life insurance is that it is tax free. His children will receive the entirety of the distribution when he dies, rather than having to give up a portion to Uncle Sam.

Single-premium life insurance is just one option to grow your funds and leave more behind for your loved ones. You can also choose to add a benefit rider to your retirement plan, so that if you don't withdraw all of the money in your account, it will go to your designated beneficiaries.

If you have a pension, then there's an even better opportunity to make a difference: You can choose to reduce the amount of money you receive monthly and designate a portion of it to a surviving family member—a gift that he or she will get for the rest of his or her life. For example, if you're entitled to $3,000 per month, you can decide to leave $1,000 per month to your grandchild. To continue paying him or her the benefit after you pass away, your pension administrator will simply reduce the amount that you get per month. That's exactly what my client Elizabeth decided to do. Elizabeth's first husband had passed away at a young age, leaving her a generous life insurance policy. She continued to work as a teacher, married again in her late thirties, and had her first and only child at age forty. As an older parent with just one child, it was important to Elizabeth to make sure that her son would receive continuous support. Since she has money saved elsewhere, she takes just a small distribution from her pension, and when she passes away, her son will receive a payment each month for as long as he lives.

Like Elizabeth, many people are becoming parents later in life. If this is the case for you, then you may want to put additional stipulations in place so that your child won't go through any funds you might leave them too quickly, or else mandate that they are to be used for a specific purpose, such as education. You should also name a custodian who could oversee any funds you leave your kids until they are old enough to manage that money on their own. It's essential to choose someone responsible, who will be there to carry out your wishes if you can't, so don't make this decision lightly.

For example, Cheryl also has only one child—a daughter named Erin, born when Cheryl was in her mid-forties. With Erin's age in mind, and the desire to control her money after she died, Cheryl reached out to her lawyer for help drafting a will and trust to designate how her assets would be used after her death. If Cheryl dies while Erin is still young, Erin will only receive a certain portion of the funds per year—with support and oversight from Cheryl's younger sister—until Erin reaches twenty-five years of age. At that point, she'll be able to spend the money as she sees fit.

SUPPORTING ORGANIZATIONS

When it comes to making end-of-life plans, you can also support causes you believe in or organizations that have played an important role in your life. My client Stephen decided to go this route. He was nearing eighty years old, his wife had passed away years earlier, and he didn't have any other family. His church had always played a big role in his life, and he credited his college with setting him up for success. So, he decided that he would divide his money between the two. Upon his death, the church will receive a portion of his assets to support its general maintenance, while the funds he's designated for his college will go toward the establishment of a scholarship in his name. Stephen is grateful for the ability to pay it forward and to help sustain the institutions that have meant so much to him throughout his life.

NO PLAN? THERE ARE CONSEQUENCES

Maybe you would like to leave money to your family, but you don't get around to making arrangements before you die. What happens then? In that scenario, your hard-earned cash goes to your estate and then gets dispersed by the courts. Strangers determine how those funds are allocated, and the process can take a very long time. If you want to ensure that your savings go to the people and places you love, then you *must* make a plan.

This is also a good time to make sure that you've designated the correct beneficiaries for any accounts you may have. I've seen too many people choose their then-spouse as their beneficiaries whenever they set up their accounts, and then forget to remove them when they're no longer together. Guess what? If your ex is the designated beneficiary on your account, then he or she will be the one getting your money when you die. If this doesn't sound appealing, check into the details on any funds you may have and make any necessary changes today.

If you've been putting off planning because you're overwhelmed, that's completely understandable. On top of the emotional difficulty that comes with thinking about your own death, it's hard to navigate it all. If you don't know where to begin, get help. You can contact a financial advisor or lawyer, who can provide assistance and refer you to other professionals for needs that fall outside of their wheelhouse. In addition, don't be afraid to ask friends, family, and colleagues for recommendations. It's often the best way to find experts in your area.

BE READY FOR TOMORROW TODAY

It's never too early to start planning for the end. None of us knows what tomorrow will bring. While it may be hard to think about, the earlier you begin planning, the more likely you'll be to achieve your goals. Here are some things to consider when making end-of-life plans:

- *Account for end-of-life expenses.* Health costs will only increase as you age, and at some point, you may no longer be able to live on your own—a very expensive proposition. Final expenses can also pose a big financial challenge. Make arrangements now to ensure that you'll get the care you need and that you won't be a burden to your family later on.

- *Determine your goals.* Do you want to have fun and indulge while you're alive, leave something behind for the ones you love and the causes you care about, or a little of both? Make sure you're clear on your goals and figure out what it will take to achieve them.

- *Check your beneficiaries—and choose wisely.* Check the current beneficiaries on your accounts. If things change and you get a divorce or decide you want your funds to go to someone else, make sure to update those recipients ASAP.

- *Seek out specialists.* End-of-life plans can be complicated. Depending on what you want to accomplish, you may need experts to help get you there—financial planners, lawyers, and others who can help guide you along the way. If you don't know of any qualified professionals, ask around. One of the best ways to find exceptional assistance is through referrals.

This is the final step. You've learned how to plant the seeds, grow your tree, and reap the fruits of your labor over the course of your life. And now you have the tools to do with that fruit what you see fit when you'll no longer need it. Whether you're using it to live your life to its fullest or seeding a new start for loved ones or a meaningful cause, you can be sure that you're doing it on your terms—and that's one of the best feelings there is.

Just like that, we're nearly at the finish line. Those in the education and public sectors have one more section of learning left to go: a chapter primarily focused on pension plans and how to make the most of them. If this doesn't apply to you, feel free to head straight to the Conclusion.

CHAPTER 10

FOR EDUCATION AND PUBLIC SECTOR PROFESSIONALS

T his last section is for those in education or public sector jobs. Many of my clients fall into this group. They're not millionaires (well, most of them aren't, anyway), but they work hard for the money they earn, and they put in the effort to make sure it serves them, too. While these industries aren't the most lucrative around, they do come with their own set of benefits—primarily pensions—and if you can make the most of them, then you can come out on top. We've touched on some of the unique opportunities and challenges that come with a pension already, but here, we'll take a deeper dive and address some additional things for you to consider if a pension is part of your benefits package.

With a pension, you're able to retire after a set number of years of service and receive a portion of your salary every year for the duration of your retirement. Pensions usually provide a significant advantage over other types of retirement funds, typically paying out far more than you put in. While you may make less than your friends and relatives working in other fields during your career, when you retire, the script usually flips. That pension continues to pay—sometimes as much as or more than your salary—for the rest of your life, as long as you treat it right. In addition, pensions offer a number of unique benefits that make them superior to other kinds of retirement plans, including:

- **Security:** Since pensions provide you with a specific income based on the number of years that you work and the salary that you earn, it's a guaranteed income stream. Other plans don't work the same way; they're based on the amount you've saved and how your investments have performed. It's a guessing game as to how much you have to put away each month and for how long you'll need to contribute to retire comfortably. There's more certainty with a pension—along with security, since the government is obligated to pay you that money.

- **COLA:** Many pension plans offer cost of living adjustments, or COLA. With these plans, for each year that you're drawing on your pension, you receive a raise to account for that ever-growing cost of living. Raises are usually about equal to inflation, which has averaged around 3 percent over the past twenty years.[61] For example, if your plan's COLA is 3 percent and you retire with a $40,000 pension, then the next year, you would get an additional

---

61 "NRTA Pension Education Toolkit: Cost of Living Adjustments (COLAs)," *National Institute on Retirement Security*, https://assets.aarp.org/www.aarp.org_/articles/work/pension-colas.pdf.

$1,200, and so on. Over time, that adds up. And it makes a big difference—especially considering everything we've discussed about inflation.

My mother has experienced the benefits of COLA in a major way. A former educator, she has been retired for more than twenty years. Each year, she gets a COLA on top of her pension, and today, she's bringing home more money than when she was working. Lots of former educators and public-sector employees find themselves in a similar position—with bigger paychecks than they had during their working days—all thanks to the COLA on their pension.

- **Early Retirement:** Your employer may offer another serious benefit when it comes to retirement: the opportunity to take it early. Many police and firefighters are given the chance to retire early, while receiving the benefits of a full pension. For instance, while it may technically take thirty years of work to get all the benefits of your pension plan, certain employees may be offered the same benefits after only twenty-five years—especially if their organization is looking for new blood. This was the case for my dad, who was an education professional. He had the opportunity to retire five years early with a full pension so that his school could hire teachers who were fresh out of school, and he was more than happy to accept.

- **Payout Options:** With pensions, you also have options in terms of how you'd like to be paid out. The most straightforward offering is to be paid your full benefit for as long as you live. But many pensions have optional survivor benefits. In this case—as we saw with Elizabeth and her son in the previous chapter—you can choose to draw a portion of your pension and leave the rest of it to your loved ones, ensuring they continue to get paid throughout their lives if you pre-decease them. If you're deciding on whether to take advantage of this opportunity, then make sure you're fully informed. The rules surrounding beneficiaries can be very technical and you usually can't change your mind once you've made your decision.

- **The opportunity to collect while you're still working:** Another beautiful thing. In many places, you can retire, begin to receive your pension, and continue to work a certain number of hours—meaning you're essentially getting paid twice.

- **Additional retirement savings opportunities:** Sometimes, you have the opportunity to invest in additional funds, too. Government organizations may offer 457(b) plans. These are similar to other retirement plans—the money you invest grows tax deferred until you take it out. But 457s are unique in that you can withdraw at any time without a penalty. That's a big deal, especially in jobs that can be grueling. I have clients who began doing maintenance work in their late teens. Because they saved regularly throughout their lives, they have been able to retire in their mid- to late-forties and receive everything they've earned, while taking a well-deserved rest. 403(b)s are another option frequently offered to employees of tax-exempt organizations such as public schools, nonprofits, and religious institutions. These plans allow for retirement and subsequent withdrawals at age fifty-five or older if the employee has left the organization—less than the 401(k) minimum of 59.5.[62]

DON'T SELL YOURSELF SHORT

As you can see, pensions can provide a lot of perks. But to get them all, you can't sell yourself short. That means knowing your plan and it's stipulations, including how long you must stay to be vested. The real key to saving well in a pension—as we've touched on throughout the book—is to start early and hang in there for the amount of time necessary to receive your full payout.

Of course, life happens and things change. But it's still important to keep your pension in mind when you're considering a move, whether it's to a different kind of job or to a similar role in another state. We've discussed this before, but I can't stress it enough: before you commit to a new plan, determine whether you're already vested in your current plan. If you're almost there, then you may want to hold out for a little longer so you can eventually claim that payout. You don't want to be a year away from getting your full benefit and throw it all away without realizing it. That's like being at the top of the ladder, a rung away from the roof, and heading straight back to the ground. If you're moving and you'll have a new pension at your next job, then be sure of the differences between your current and future plans, since pensions differ from state to state.

One other thing to note: If you're young and thinking about taking some time away to raise children, don't pull out your contribution. You can usually pick right up where you left off when you're

---

62   "403(b) Plan," *Investopedia*, www.investopedia.com/terms/1/403bplan.asp.

ready to come back, without losing any of the progress you've made. But that's not the case if you take out everything you put in.

BOOST YOUR SALARY FOR BIGGER REWARDS

You should also work to increase your salary as much as possible, because your pension is usually based on your best earning years. That may mean taking on more responsibilities that also pay more. For example, if you work in a school, you might sign on to be department chair, provide after-school tutoring, or coach a sport to boost your income.

For educators, attaining additional schooling often comes with a salary bump—which will help increase your pension, as well. But first you need to figure out whether it will pay off for you. You have to weigh the potential salary benefit against the cost of any program you're considering, including how long it will take you to pay off the loans you'd have to take out to attend. For instance, if you'd need to borrow $60,000 to get a master's degree in special education—at an eventual cost of $120,000 when you add interest to the equation—then you may find that, based on the kind of raises you'd get, you'd never make up the difference. On the other hand, if that schooling will put you on track for a raise, followed by a promotion or two that would bump up your pay grade year after year, then it may very well be worth your original investment.

TAP INTO AVAILABLE RESOURCES

While you can create challenges for yourself if you don't pay attention to your plan's provisions or pull out money too soon, when you use these tools to the fullest, they can be a real boon in retirement. Make sure you're informed about anything and everything that's available to you when you're just getting started, so that you can make the best possible decisions (we've seen what happens when you don't). And don't worry; you don't have to go it alone. There are plenty of resources to help you manage a pension. Your state's pension website and handbook can be great sources of information, as can any seminars offered by your district. Many pension plans also provide the opportunity to meet one-on-one with your provider to discuss your individual case, especially as you age.

If you're proactive, pensions can be an incredible benefit. Learn about your plan from the start and put in the time and effort to make the most of it. If you do, you're almost guaranteed to find yourself in a great position down the line—which brings us to the end of ours.

CONCLUSION

T hroughout this book, you've seen that living a healthy financial life doesn't have to be complicated. The stories and principles we've discussed demonstrate that success is about your net worth, not necessarily your income. If you know your goals, you can figure out how to get there using three basic strategies: living below your means, managing taxes, and beating inflation. It's as simple as that. Pay attention to the amount of money you spend and save, and use the concepts we discussed to protect yourself and your family in case you live too long or die too soon.

If you do slip up, there's usually time to get back on track, as long as you confront the situation and get the help you need. And if you're doing well and meeting your goals, then reward yourself. Being smart financially doesn't always have to be a slog.

Once you've put these strategies to work, you can look for additional resources to expand your knowledge. While there are thousands of resources out there written on financial literacy, I like *Money* magazine and *Kiplinger's* for straightforward personal finance advice, as well as books like *The Richest Man in Babylon* by George

Samuel Classon, which explains basic financial concepts through a series of ancient parables, and *The Millionaire Next Door*, by Thomas J. Stanley. These have stood the test of time, keeping it simple while conveying essential money principles. You can also look out for financial literacy courses nearby—local libraries, community centers, and colleges usually offer them.

I'm also a big believer in the idea that you model the behavior of the company you keep. If you have a family member, friend, or coworker who seems to have their financial life together, talk to them about how they've created their current situation. They may also be able to refer you to professionals in your area that can help you get on track. On that note, never be afraid to reach out to an expert. While, on the surface, working with a financial advisor is about addressing money issues and setting yourself up for stability, it's also about making your life easier. When your financial house is in order, your problems don't go away, but they do become much smaller. That means you can do and appreciate more. Without financial stressors, you can truly enjoy your existence, pursue meaningful work, and give back to your family and your community. Like seeing a mechanic or a trusted physician, a financial advisor can help you maintain your financial health and address any problems that may arise.

To do that, you may have to put your pride aside and be honest about any unproductive habits or difficulties. Know that everyone has faced a financial challenge at some point in their lives. I've had my own financial ups and downs. I've been in credit card debt, loaned people money and haven't been paid back, made investments that weren't the best, and bought unnecessary items. It's human to make mistakes, but seeking help can be the difference between a financial disaster and a full recovery.

The key is to live and learn, and it's part of why I'm so passionate about what I do. I got into this field to help people. I've worked with thousands of individuals and families over the course of my career. I've helped them create financial blueprints that they can build their lives around. Years down the line, it's amazing to view the end product. Along the way, we've set goals for each stage they've gone through, seen ups and downs, and talked through the times when they wanted to quit. It's incredibly gratifying when my clients call me to let me know that the work we've done together has helped to improve their lives in one way or another.

Every day, I have the opportunity to talk to clients who have made amazing strides—families who can afford to send their kids to college, and men and women who can retire on their own terms and live the kind of life they want. I hear from people facing difficult personal situations, like the loss of a spouse. They call me in tears, grateful that they won't have to worry about their finances in addition to dealing with their loss. Still others call to share that they're able to access the care they need as they age and leave behind a legacy that they're proud of. That impact is exponential; my clients have the opportunity to talk to and teach their family, friends, and colleagues about finances too.

With the resources in this book, you have those opportunities as well. I hope they serve you and your community, and that this is a tool you turn to time and again to build a happy, healthy, and financially sound life. You can do it, and I'm rooting for you.

"The habit of saving is itself an education; it fosters every virtue, teaches self-denial, cultivates the sense of order, trains to forethought, and so broadens the mind." —T.T. Munger

ABOUT THE AUTHOR

As the owner of Melan Financial for more than two decades, Mitch Melan is committed to providing trustworthy and responsible advice to his clients. He considers himself a financial coach, having helped thousands of individuals work toward and achieve their financial goals.

Mitch began his career as an elementary school teacher in the Atlanta Public Schools system, teaching himself smart money principles to make the most of his earnings and build a sound financial life. Realizing he had a passion for saving and investing—and for helping others—Mitch became a financial advisor, building a practice that supports many middle-class Americans in their efforts to live comfortably.

Mitch has received a number of awards and accolades for his work. He was inducted into the Lincoln Investment Hall of Fame[63]

---

63 The Hall of Fame recognizes those Lincoln Investment financial advisors who have achieved the firm's annual qualifying criteria at least 10 times based on overall production, new clients, advisory accounts and assets. Lincoln Investment honors them for their dedication to helping people retire well by inducting them into its Hall of Fame.

and has been rated a Five-Star Wealth Manager by Five Star Professional and *Atlanta* magazine, an accolade recognizing less than 2 percent of licensed wealth managers in the area.[64] The ranking is based on integrity, customer service, value of the services provided, and the quality of his recommendations. Mitch lives metro Atlanta with his wife and two children.

---

64   The Five Star Wealth Manager award, administered by Crescendo Business Services, LLC (dba Five Star Professional), is based on 10 objective criteria:
   a) Credentialed as an investment advisory representative (IAR) or a registered investment advisor;
   b) Actively employed as a credentialed professional in the financial services industry for a minimum of five years;
   c) Favorable regulatory and complaint history review;
   d) Fulfilled their firm review based on internal firm standards;
   e) Accepting new clients;
   f) One-year client retention rate;
   g) Five-year client retention rate;
   h) Non-institutionalized discretionary and/or non-discretionary client assets administered;
   i) Number of client households served;
   j) Educational and professional designations.
   Wealth managers do not pay a fee to be considered or awarded.
   Once awarded, wealth managers may opt to purchase additional profile ad space or related award promotional products. The award methodology does not evaluate the quality of services provided. The award is not indicative of the award winner's future performance. More than 7,500 Atlanta wealth managers were considered for the award; less than 2 percent of the award candidates were named Five Star Wealth Managers.
   To qualify as having a favorable regulatory and complaint history for this award, the person cannot have (1) been subject to a regulatory action that resulted in a license being suspended or revoked, or payment of a fine, (2) had more than a total of three customer complaints files against them (settled or pending) with any regulatory authority of Five Star Professional's customer complaint process, (3) individually contributed to a financial settlement of a customer complaint filed with a regulatory authority, (4) filed for bankruptcy, or (5) been convicted of a felony.

9 781949 639773